THE WASPS

Ann Arbor
Science
Library

The Wasps

*by Howard E. Evans and
Mary Jane West Eberhard*

Drawings by Sarah Landry

ANN ARBOR

THE UNIVERSITY OF MICHIGAN PRESS

Copyright © by The University of Michigan 1970
All rights reserved
ISBN 0–472–05018–4 (paperbound)
ISBN 0–472–00118–3 (clothbound)
Library of Congress Catalog Card No. 71–124448
Published in the United States of America by
The University of Michigan Press and simultaneously
in Don Mills, Canada, by Longmans Canada Limited
Manufactured in the United States of America

Contents

1 . *Introduction*

Wasps are not the most popular of animals, for it is hard for us to reconcile ourselves to creatures so well equipped to defend themselves. Yet there are few organisms whose presence on earth is so fortunate from our point of view. There are some four thousand species of wasps in the United States alone, and in the world as a whole they number in the tens of thousands of species. With a few minor exceptions, wasps develop as parasites or predators on other arthropods, often on plant-feeding insects that compete with us for the bounty of the earth. Their role in the natural control of pest insects is difficult to document, for they perform their roles unheralded and often unnoticed. But it has been said of the Hymenoptera (the insect order into which wasps fall) as a whole that man could scarcely survive without their assistance in regulating the populations of plant-feeding insects. This evaluation includes not only true wasps, but also the so-called "parasitic Hymenoptera," which we shall discuss briefly later in this chapter.

Furthermore, wasps provide admirable subjects for studies of animal behavior, that most underdeveloped and yet critically important facet of biology. The solitary wasps display elaborate, relatively stereotyped behavior patterns that are readily amenable to description and analysis, while subsocial and social wasps exhibit various stages in the evolution of sociality more clearly than any other group of organisms. This book will emphasize wasp behavior, but in this introductory chapter we would first like to say a few more words about the importance of wasps to man and then present a brief survey of the Hymenoptera, with particular attention to the major groups of wasps. With this background, we may then turn to a consideration of their ways of living.

Wasps and Man

Despite the authors' admiration for wasps, we would be the last to deny that they can sting. Indeed, in the course of our studies we have had all too many occasions to confirm that fact. The venom is injected via a needle-like projection from the tail end of the body, usually called simply "the sting." Its effects vary from scarcely perceptible to almost unbearably severe pain. While the pain is usually localized at the site of the puncture, there may be various systemic effects, and some persons develop strong allergies to the venom. It is said that from 15 to 20 persons die each year in the United States as a result of anaphylactic shock following the stings of wasps, bees, and other Hymenoptera. This figure does not, of course, include undiagnosed cases or deaths caused indirectly, for example by traffic accidents caused by wasps or bees that sting or frighten the drivers of cars. Yellow jackets and common paper wasps often nest around our homes, and when their nests are disturbed they defend them vigorously, making liberal use of a powerful venom which is a mixture of enzymes and proteins, including such substances as serotonin and histamine. It is little wonder that the reaction of most persons to wasps is one of fear and revulsion.

Yet on the whole the danger of wasps has been exaggerated. The vast majority—perhaps 90% of the known species—are solitary kinds that have venom of quite a different nature, often producing momentary pain but nothing more; furthermore, many wasps are so small that they are unable or barely able to pierce the skin. Solitary wasps are not aggressive and usually do not even attempt to defend their nests. Except in a few tropical social wasps, the sting does not remain in the wound, with the poison sac attached, as it does when a honeybee stings. Finally, it must be remembered that since the sting is a modified ovipositor (egg-laying tube), only the females are able to sting. This does not mean that one should not maintain a healthy respect for wasps, but it does mean that he should not let this respect blind him to the fascination of their modes of life or to the important role they play in killing noxious insects.

On several occasions solitary wasps have been introduced into new areas to assist in the biological control of pests. A digger wasp, *Larra americana,* was introduced into Puerto Rico from South America many years ago, and it is well established and important in the control of mole crickets in sugar cane fields. The wasp *Scolia manilae* was imported from the Philippines to Hawaii, where it brought about quick and effective control of the larvae of the Oriental beetle, a serious pest in cane fields (Fig. 1). When the Japanese beetle was a major plague in the northeastern United States, the United States Department of Agriculture imported several species of *Tiphia* from Japan and released them in numbers for

FIG. 1. *Scolia manilae,* a wasp introduced into Hawaii to control white grubs. The female (left) has a robust body and 12-segmented antennae, while the male (right) has a much more slender body and 13-segmented antennae. These features distinguish the sexes in most wasps, although in some the sexual dimorphism is more extreme. (F.X. Williams, 1919).

the control of that insect (Fig. 10). The value of solitary wasps in biological control has been overshadowed by that of the parasitic Hymenoptera, but they remain of potential value for introduction into new areas, and of course as major factors in the natural control of pests throughout the world. Their usefulness as control agents is reduced by the fact that most require special conditions for nesting; but balanced against that is the fact that nearly all are highly host-specific and very few attack beneficial insects.

Many social wasps also prey upon insects of economic importance, and in some agricultural regions these wasps are considered valuable control agents. For example, *Ropalidia gregaria* nests in cane fields in the Philippines, where it destroys the sugar cane leafhopper. In the West Indies, the so-called "Spanish Jack" or "Jack Spaniel," a species of *Polistes,* is rated highly for its role in preying on various leaf-feeding caterpillars, particularly the cotton leafworm. In the southeastern United States, species of *Polistes* have been found to reduce substantially the population levels of tobacco hornworms, especially when suitable nesting shelters were placed in the fields. However, some social wasps must go on record as economic pests themselves. Several species have been observed systematically raiding honeybee hives. In British Guiana *Synoeca surinama* captures honeybee workers at the entrances to hives; and *Mischocyttarus drewseni* makes sustained attacks on "weak" hives, in which nurse bees are scarce and some advanced brood cells uncapped, procuring honey and brood. *Vespa* and *Polistes* species are also recorded as pests of apiaries.

Most, if not all, social wasps collect nectar, and some of them store appreciable amounts of it in the nest (see Chapter V). Perhaps the most famous of the honey-storing wasps are those of the genus *Brachygastra* (formerly called *Nectarina*). In Brazil the honey of *Brachygastra lecheguana* is gathered from large nests, usually during the Brazilian summer. If the base of the nest is left on the branch the inhabitants rebuild it in the same place, and the colony can be exploited again the next year. In Mexico the honey of *B. lecheguana* has commercial value. Wasp farmers—they could properly be called "vespiculturists"— gather young nests and transplant them to places where they can be protected, then periodically oust the inhabitants from the nest with smoke, destroy the nest to obtain the honey, and allow the wasps to return and rebuild the colony. *Polybia occidentalis* is also used as a source of edible honey in Mexico. Consumers of wasp honey are well-advised to patronize a trustworthy vespiculturist, for the honey of *B. lecheguana* is occasionally poisonous because of the incorporation of nectar from certain flowers.

The grublike larvae of social wasps are commonly used as fishing bait in many parts of the world. In some places they are even consumed, raw or fried, by humans. A University of Texas anthropologist discovered that the Chuh Indians, a small group of Mayans living in northwestern Guatemala, collect *Polistes* nests and eat the pupae. They believe that people who eat the young of these wasps will have children with big eyes like those of the wasps. This idea may have been suggested by the stark black eyes of the *Polistes* pupa which are a striking contrast with the snowy white bodies as the pupa begins to develop pigment. From a purely practical point of view it is surprising that the brood of social wasps are not more commonly cooked and eaten by human beings, since a colony constitutes a rich source of protein food requiring little cultivation. Baked wasp grubs were earnestly recommended by Vincent Holt in his 1885 book *Why Not Eat Insects?*:

"What disciple of old Izaak Walton, when he has been all the morning enticing the wily trout with luscious wasp grubs baked to a turn, has not suspected a new and appetizing taste imparted to his midday meal of bread and cheese or sandwich? . . . Having no prejudices against insect food, I have myself spread the baked grubs upon my bread, and found their excellent flavour quite sufficient to account for the fondness of the trout for this particular bait."

A Brief Survey of the Hymenoptera

Wasps make up part of the insect order Hymenoptera, a group of enormous size, with more than 100,000 described species. The order also contains two groups of insects that clearly evolved from wasps but are so different in appearance that they are called by different names: the ants and the bees. It also includes two other large groups which fall outside the scope of this book: the sawflies and the parasitoids. Sawflies are plant-feeders which have a rather generalized structure and lack the "wasp waist" of most Hymenoptera. Although usually called sawflies in the United States because of their sawlike ovipositor, they are of course not true flies, and are perhaps better called leaf wasps, wood wasps, and stem wasps, as they are in some parts of the world. The parasitoids are sometimes called parasitic wasps or "parasitic Hymenoptera"; they make up an enormous group of insects, many of which develop as parasites of other insects. Included in this group are the ichneumons, the chalcid wasps, and a major group of plant pests, the gall wasps. This book is concerned only with the "true wasps" (those having a fully developed sting), but these can best be understood in the context of the Hymenoptera as a whole.

The sawflies (suborder Symphyta, meaning "living with plants") are clearly the most primitive Hymenoptera. The adults have the most complete wing venation of any Hymenoptera, and the larvae retain at least some evidence of legs (Fig. 2). Also, the lack of specializations such as the "wasp waist" suggests that these insects are closest to the ancestral stock of the Hymenoptera. The earliest fossils assignable to this order, from the Triassic,

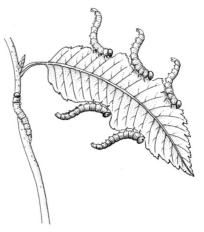

FIG. 2. The caterpillarlike larvae of a leaf-feeding sawfly or leaf-wasp. When disturbed, these larvae often assume the slightly coiled position shown in this drawing.

nearly two hundred million years ago, appear to be related to *Xyela,* a genus of leaf wasps the living members of which feed on the staminate flowers of pines. The earliest fossil wood wasps occur in Jurassic strata, and these are related to genera which now bore in conifers. Many living leaf and wood wasps attack relatively primitive groups of plants, including ferns, conifers, Salicaceae, and Rosaceae. The stem wasps bore in the stems of grasses

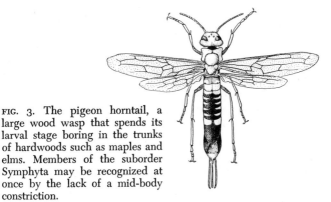

FIG. 3. The pigeon horntail, a large wood wasp that spends its larval stage boring in the trunks of hardwoods such as maples and elms. Members of the suborder Symphyta may be recognized at once by the lack of a mid-body constriction.

and include such pests as the wheat stem sawfly; the structure of these wasps suggests that they are most like the insects that gave rise to the parasitic Hymenoptera.

The stem wasps (Cephidae) show the initial stages of a constriction between the first two abdominal segments, a constriction that is carried to completion in the second and much larger suborder of Hymenoptera, the Apocrita (from the Greek, meaning "separated"). This constriction, or "wasp waist," is of major adaptive significance, since it enables the females to direct the posterior portion of their bodies freely in several directions; in the act of egg-laying or stinging it is often directed forward beneath the body, enabling the wasp to make use of its organs of sight, touch, and smell while performing this critical and often lightning-fast behavior. The vast majority of Apocrita are entomophagous (i.e., insect-eating), although members of several groups have returned secondarily to a plant diet (Fig. 14). The earliest fossil parasitic Hymenoptera (or Terebrantia, from the Latin word *terebra,* "drill") appear in rocks dating from the Jurassic period, somewhat later than the first Symphyta and somewhat earlier than the first true wasps and ants. The parasitic wasps share certain generalized structural features with the sawflies which are not found in the true wasps, and this fact plus the longer fossil record leads us to believe that the Terebrantia occupy an evolutionary position intermediate between the Symphyta and the Aculeata (or stinging Hymenoptera). However, all existing parasitic Hymenoptera are much too specialized to have been ancestral to the true wasps.

Before passing on to the insects that provide the major subjects of this book, a few words should be said about the life histories of the parasitic Hymenoptera, for in some measure these may approximate the ancestral type of the Aculeata. In fact, the group is so large and diverse that generalization is difficult. Adult parasitic Hymenoptera (like many adult Symphyta) often take nourishment from dew, honeydew, and the nectar of flowers; however, the females of some species oviposit into a host, then feed on the host's blood at the site of the egg-laying puncture. In many instances, the female possesses poison glands which discharge through the ovipositor, permitting her to immobilize the host while the egg or eggs are laid. However, the host typically recovers in a short time and goes about its normal activities with the parasitic larva or larvae developing on or within it. In most cases, the parasite is smaller than its host and several to many develop at the expense of one host, causing its eventual death.

As may be readily seen, these insects are not parasites in the usual sense, since they destroy their host; more properly, they are highly efficient predators which slowly devour a single host rather than consuming a series of individuals. Many years ago the Finnish entomologist O.M. Reuter proposed the word "parasitoid" to describe this unusual mode of life. Parasitoids resemble predators in having free-living adults that seek out a series of hosts; they resemble parasites in the close attachment of their larvae to the host and in their relatively high degree of host-specificity, that is, the majority of species attack only one particular kind of arthropod. For example, the ichneumon wasp *Megarhyssa* (Fig. 4) locates the larvae of certain wood wasps deep in the trunks of trees, and by means of its long ovipositor inserts an egg upon the larva. In this case the diameter of the egg is greater than that of the thread-like ovipositor, and the egg is drawn out into a slender filament as it is laid. When it is released, the yolk flows into one portion of the filament, forming a robust egg with a very thin "tail." The larva of *Megarhyssa* develops slowly on the host, feeding on blood and soft tissues and destroying the vital organs only after the wood wasp larva has cut its way nearly to the surface of the wood, as it normally does just before pupating. Here the *Megarhyssa* pupates, and the emerging adult is able to

FIG. 4. The parasitic wasp *Megarhyssa* inserting her ovipositor through the trunk of a tree preparatory to laying her egg on a pigeon horntail larva deep inside the tree.

emerge with a minimum of boring. Beautiful adaptations such as this are common among parasitoids, which must be closely synchronized to the life cycle and activities of the host in order to thrive.

Quite a few "parasitic Hymenoptera" have reverted to a plant-feeding diet, such as the clover seed chalcid, the wheat jointworm, and several other pest species. Most conspicuous are the great numbers of gall wasps which form globular or irregular growths on bushes and trees, especially oaks. Yet the majority of chalcid wasps and even many "gall wasps" are parasitoids, and we may feel sure that the phytophagous members of these groups have reverted to plants secondarily.

True wasps differ from parasitoids in having the ovipositor fully modified for injecting venom into the host: it has become a sting, and the egg no longer passes down it, but is discharged directly from the body. Another curious feature of true wasps and of ants and bees is that the number of antennal segments has become fixed at thirteen or slightly fewer. In the majority the females have twelve antennal segments and the males thirteen, thus providing a nice feature for identifying these as Aculeata (from the Latin *aculeus*, a sting) and determining the sex at the same time. Of course, only the females are provided with stings, so the sex is determinable on this basis, sometimes painfully so. There is reason to regard the ants as specialized derivatives of primitive wasps, while bees are believed to represent a group of more highly developed wasps which have become adapted for exploiting the nectar and pollen of flowers as food. Thus the bees, like some ants and a very few true wasps, have reverted to a diet of plant products like their remote ancestors, the Symphyta. The first bees appear in the fossil record in the Tertiary, some fifty million years ago. Wasps and ants are now known from the Cretaceous period, roughly 100 million years ago. Some of the earliest fossil wasps are strikingly like modern forms, suggesting that the major steps in wasp evolution occurred in the late Mesozoic.

Ants may be recognized by the fact that one or two segments behind the usual mid-body constriction are separated off as small nodes or scales (Fig. 5). Bees may be distinguished from wasps by their robust bodies covered with hairs, many of which are plumed (Fig. 6). However, some bees which are not pollen-gatherers but parasites of other bees have short body hairs and are difficult to tell at a glance from wasps. In this case, one must rely upon a close examination of the hind tarsus (basal section of the terminal part of the leg), which in all bees is at least slightly more swollen than it is in wasps. There are some excellent books on ants and on bees, and we shall say no more about them here.

The true wasps inherited the parasitoid mode of life, and some of the more generalized kinds behave essentially as parasitoids except that their sting no longer functions as an ovipositor. But the majority of wasps paralyze their hosts more or less permanently by stinging them, then carry them to a crevice or to a specially prepared nest where the egg is laid and larval development takes place.

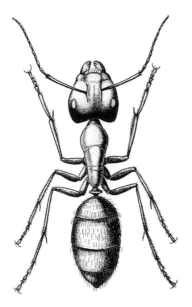

FIG. 5. A worker carpenter ant. Male ants, and also most queens during their mating flight, have well developed wings. However, all ants may be distinguished by the one or two nodes between the second and third of the three major body parts.

The sting apparatus and accompanying poison glands undoubtedly evolved as a means of supplying the larva with immobile but well preserved food. Secondarily, they serve the females well in self-defense. However, in the higher, social wasps, such as the yellow jackets, the sting no longer serves a role in immobilizing the prey, which is seized and chewed up with the mandibles. In these wasps different venoms have evolved, the sting is often barbed, and the sting apparatus has become an effective weapon for defending the communal nest against predators, especially vertebrate animals.

Adult wasps feed primarily on nectar and other plant juices, although some females do feed to a limited extent on the prey they capture. However, since most prey is fed directly to the offspring, or at least placed in the nest for their consumption, and since most wasps are rather highly

FIG. 6. A bee, showing the robust, hairy body and the modifications of the legs for carrying pollen. This is a stingless bee, one of the most advanced groups of Hymenoptera.

host-specific (another trait inherited from the parasitoids), it is perhaps stretching a point to call them predators. Also, it must be remembered that the males lack a sting and play no role in the nesting process; they feed exclusively on dew, honeydew, and the nectar of flowers, and are not predators by any definition. The unique female-limited, host-specific, and next-generation-oriented predation of wasps has sometimes been referred to as "predatoidism", to emphasize its evolution from parasitoidism. This term has not been widely used and will not be used again here, but one should not forget the several unusual features of the predatory behavior of these insects.

The Major Groups of Wasps

The wasps are an exceedingly diverse group both in structure and in behavior. Some are less than an eighth of an inch in length, while others measure more than three inches and have a wingspan of four inches or more. Some have wingless females which may be mistaken for ants, and some robust, hairy kinds are often called "bees," although in each case the resemblance is superficial. Collectively wasps prey upon almost every kind of insect as well as upon spiders. Their nests may be simple, temporary affairs or exceedingly complex structures elaborated by a great many co-operating individuals and lasting for many months. Some make no nests at all, either because they behave as parasitoids or because they have become parasites using the nests of other wasps or of bees. We shall take a closer look at the natural history of wasps in the next chapter. First, we must take a brief look at some of the major groups, for the wasps comprise several distinct families, some of them containing literally thousands of species. Only a few general remarks are offered here; a good textbook such as that of Imms (revised edition, 1957), should be consulted for further details.

It cannot be said that the true wasps are sharply separated from the parasitic wasps on the basis of either structure or behavior. One family of rather rare insects, the Trigonalidae, has been shifted back and forth between the two groups; these insects have antennae of much more than thirteen segments, as well as other parasitoid features, but their ovipositor and wing venation are more of the form of the true wasps. In behavior, they appear to be aberrant parasitoids. Another family of poorly known, tropical wasps, the Sclerogibbidae, also has parasitoid habits and twenty or more antennal segments, although in other respects these resemble true wasps. Otherwise the wasps are reasonably well defined and often grouped into five superfamilies, although unfortunately not all families fit snugly into one of the superfamilies. The two super-families universally considered most primitive are the Scolioidea and the Bethyloidea. There are two relict fam-ilies which occur in the southern hemisphere and which appear to bridge the gap between these two superfami-lies: the Scolebythidae and the Plumariidae. Nothing is known about the biology of either group, and they need not concern us further here.

The bethyloid wasps (superfamily Bethyloidea) are often considered lowest in the scale of wasp evolution, since the majority of them behave as parasitoids. Females of the family Dryinidae have the front tarsi modified to form a traplike device for capturing leafhoppers and re-lated insects (Fig. 7). The egg is laid inside the abdomen of the host, and development of the larva is at first inter-nal. These are the only Aculeata known to oviposit and develop inside the host, although this is common among the Terebrantia. The Bethylidae attack the larvae of bee-

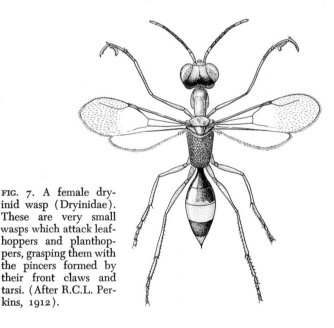

FIG. 7. A female dry-inid wasp (Dryinidae). These are very small wasps which attack leaf-hoppers and planthop-pers, grasping them with the pincers formed by their front claws and tarsi. (After R.C.L. Per-kins, 1912).

tles and of moths living in hidden situations, such as in the soil, in burrows in wood, leaf mines and galls, etc. These are minute wasps, the females often wingless and sometimes blind (Fig. 27). They are usually much smaller than their hosts, and the female typically lays several eggs on the host and several larvae develop on it. This, again, is a common feature of true parasitoids, but the majority of wasps are larger than their hosts and use several to feed a single larva. Bethylidae are provided with surprisingly potent stings for their size, and the stings of certain species have been reported to produce systemic effects in man. Bethylids usually leave their host *in situ,* but some species have been observed to drag their large prey to a crevice, which is then sealed off.

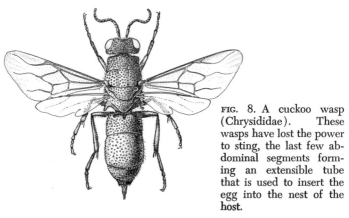

FIG. 8. A cuckoo wasp (Chrysididae). These wasps have lost the power to sting, the last few abdominal segments forming an extensible tube that is used to insert the egg into the nest of the host.

Another family of Bethyloidea is the Chrysididae, or cuckoo wasps. These are generally brilliantly blue, green, or reddish in color, and have a thick, heavily sculptured integument (Fig. 8). Their abdomen is short and is concave beneath, so that it is capable of being turned beneath the thorax (the middle region of the body) and applied against it to form a tight, hard ball (Fig. 104). This is believed to be a device for escaping the stings of their hosts, for the majority of cuckoo wasps lay their eggs in the nests of wasps and bees, and their larvae develop as parasites of those insects (Chapter VI).

Scolioid wasps (superfamily Scolioidea) are relatively short-legged, hairy and spiny wasps, many of them of moderate to large size (Figs. 1, 9). Members of the families Tiphiidae and Scoliidae attack beetle larvae in the ground, usually leaving the larva *in situ* but sometimes moving it to a more suitable niche or even preparing a cell to receive it. Some groups of Tiphiidae have wingless females which are smaller and very different in appearance from the males; in some cases the male carries the female about during a prolonged mating flight (Fig. 27). In the Mutillidae the females are always wingless and often brilliantly colored; these are the so-called "velvet ants," noted for their painful stings (Figs. 59, 105). Most Mutillidae are parasites of wasps and bees, and they are often abundant in areas where their hosts are nesting. Members of the family Sapygidae are fully winged in both sexes; these are generally less common than Mutillidae but like them are parasites of other Aculeata, chiefly of bees that nest in hollow twigs.

The vespoid wasps (superfamily Vespoidea) are familiar to everyone, for this group includes the yellow jackets,

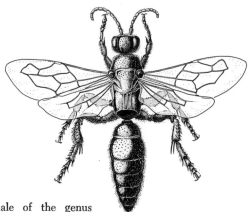

FIG. 9. A female of the genus *Tiphia* (Tiphiidae).

FIG. 10. The larva of *Tiphia* feeding on a grub of the Japanese beetle. Top figure, a young larva that has fed for only a day or two. Lower figure, a nearly mature larva that has almost consumed the grub. (U.S. Department of Agriculture).

FIG. 11. A mason wasp (Eumenidae). This is a female *Ancistrocerus antilope* at the entrance of a "trap nest" (see Chapter III). Note that the wings appear very slender, a result of the fact that they are folded longitudinally.

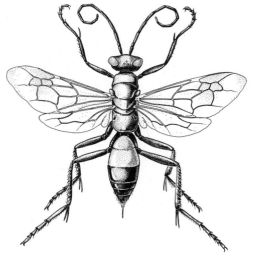

FIG. 12. A spider wasp, *Calicurgus* (Pompilidae). The unusually long legs help to distinguish these wasps, all of which prey upon spiders.

the hornets (a name applied to larger members of the same general group), and the paper wasps common around our homes (Figs. 78, 102). These are social wasps (family Vespidae), that is, they live in colonies composed mostly of sterile workers and containing one or more egg-laying queens and, at certain seasons, numerous males or drones. Social wasps are especially abundant in the tropics, although the yellow jackets are primarily a temperate or even subarctic group. Besides the social wasps, the Vespoidea includes the Masaridae, which are much less

FIG. 13. A digger wasp, *Stictia carolina* (Sphecidae). The mandibles, here slightly extended, are used to loosen firm soil, while the front legs are used for scraping the soil back beneath the body. The front legs are curved toward the midline of the body, bringing the spines of the "tarsal rake" in contact with the substrate.

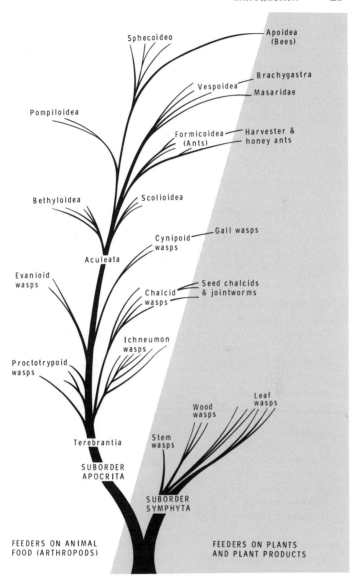

FIG. 14. Dendrogram showing the probable evolution of the major groups of Hymenoptera.

often encountered and which are unusual in that many of them store their nests not with insect food but with nectar and pollen. The family Eumenidae is much larger and includes a diverse assortment of predators on the larvae of moths and beetles. Some of the Eumenidae nest in the ground, some in hollow twigs, and some in free mud nests; nearly all of them use mud at some stage in the nesting process, hence the name "mason wasps," which is often applied to these insects (Fig. 11). The Vespoidea as a whole tend to fold their forewings longitudinally when at rest, making them appear narrower than usual (with some

OUTLINE OF THE CLASSIFICATION OF THE MAJOR GROUPS OF WASPS

Family	No. of species[1]	Representative genera
Superfamily Bethyloidea		
Bethylidae	300	*Pristocera, Epyris*
Dryinidae	300	*Chelogynus, Gonatopus*
Chrysididae (Cuckoo wasps)	200	*Chrysis, Parnopes*
Superfamily Scolioidea		
Tiphiidae	200	*Tiphia, Methocha*
Scoliidae	30	*Scolia, Campsomeris*
Mutillidae (Velvet ants)	500	*Dasymutilla, Ephuta*
Sapygidae	30	*Sapyga, Eusapyga*
Superfamily Vespoidea		
Eumenidae (Mason wasps)	350	*Eumenes, Ancistrocerus, Synagris, Zethus*
Masaridae	25	*Pseudomasaris, Euparagia*
Vespidae (Paper wasps, Yellow Jackets, Hornets)	30	*Polistes, Polybia, Ropalidia, Vespula*
Superfamily Pompiloidea		
Rhopalosomatidae	2	*Rhopalosoma, Olixon*
Pompilidae (Spider wasps)	300	*Pepsis, Pompilus Ceropales, Evagetes*
Superfamily Sphecoidea	1400	*Sphex, Ammophila,*
Sphecidae (Digger wasps)		*Bembix, Philanthus*

1. Approximate number occurring in America north of Mexico.

exceptions); the name "plaited-winged wasps" is sometimes applied to the superfamily.

The pompiloid wasps (Pompiloidea) include the large family Pompilidae, the spider wasps (Fig. 12). These are long-legged, very active wasps which prey on spiders of approximately their own size, for (unlike other spider predators among the Sphecidae) they use a single spider per nest-cell. Like Sphecidae, but unlike Scolioidea and Vespoidea, the posterior, lateral lobes of the pronotum (on the back just behind the head) form rounded lobes, but in the spider wasps these lobes touch the anterior wing-bases, while in Sphecidae they do not. A small family of rarely encountered cricket-predators, the Rhopalo-somatidae, is sometimes also included in the Pompiloidea.

By far the largest group of wasps is the Sphecidae, the sole family of Sphecoidea (Fig. 13). The majority of Sphecidae dig nests in the soil, and for this reason they are called "digger wasps," although a fair number nest in rotten wood or stems and a few make nests of mud or other materials. Sphecidae vary tremendously in size and appearance, and they are also exceedingly diverse in their nesting behavior. Although digger wasps are primarily solitary nesters, some species nest in large aggregations, and a very few live in simple co-operative societies. We shall have a great deal more to say about various digger wasps in the two chapters that follow.

II. *The Natural History of Wasps*

Like many other insects, wasps undergo complete meta-
morphosis, and have four life stages: egg, larva, pupa, and
adult. Without exception, the first three stages are spent
in a nest or upon another arthropod, so they are rarely observed except by specialists. Yet most wasps spend much
more time in the immature stages than as adults, and
much of the adult life is devoted to preparation for the
survival of the eggs and larvae of the next generation. In
this chapter we shall discuss the immature stages briefly
and then turn our attention to some of the more general
activities of the adults, especially those performed away
from the nest.

The Egg Stage

The eggs of wasps are whitish, sausage-shaped and protected by only a very delicate pellicle. The majority are
attached externally to an immobilized arthropod, either by
one end or for the greater part of their length. As already
mentioned, the Dryinidae are exceptional in laying the
egg internally in their leafhopper or planthopper host, and
the Bethylidae are exceptional in that some of them lay
several eggs on one host (up to seven or eight, rarely as
many as sixteen). Certain bethylids are reported to lay
more eggs on larger hosts than on smaller ones, while
some are reported to lay more eggs per host under conditions of host scarcity.

24

In other wasps a single egg is deposited on the prey, and the position of the egg tends to be relatively constant in a given species, often within a genus or group of genera. Many members of the families Scoliidae and Tiphiidae attack white grubs (the larvae of June beetles); in the former group, the egg is laid in an erect position, while in the latter it is glued closely to the integument after an extensive kneading of the body surface of the paralyzed grub, and members of one species tend to lay their egg at one particular point. Most Pompilidae and Sphecidae also lay the egg at quite a specific place on their prey; examples are shown in Figures 15 and 16.

The position in which the egg is laid is of considerable adaptive significance, for the newly hatched larva normally begins to feed without moving about. In the case of hardbodied arthropods, the anterior end of the egg is usually located at a coxal cavity or some other weak point in the integument. In some Sphecidae, the egg is attached to the host by its posterior end only and is in an oblique or erect position, so that the emerging larva is free to move its head about and reach various prey in the cell.

Oviposition in the empty nest-cell, before any prey is brought in, has developed independently in several stocks of Sphecidae. In some species the egg is fastened in an oblique or erect position in the bottom of the cell, while in others it is laid loosely in the bottom of the cell or against a wall. All Vespoidea oviposit in the empty cell before prey is introduced. Many Eumenidae deposit an egg which has a delicate filament at one end, and the egg is suspended by this filament from the top or side of the cell. Other Vespoidea lay the egg loosely in the cell or glue it to a wall; the latter method is characteristic of the social species.

In solitary wasps, the egg stage is of short duration, commonly only two or three days, but in social wasps it is much longer (two weeks or more). Just prior to hatching

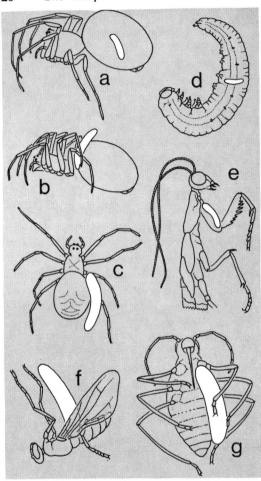

FIG. 15. Eggs of various Pompilidae and Sphecidae on prey. *a,* egg of *Episyron quinquenotatus* (Pompilidae) on *Araneus* spider (Evans, 1963). *b,* egg of *Nitelopterus evansi* (Sphecidae) on *Dictyna* spider (Evans, 1963). *c,* egg of *Sceliphron tubifex* (Sphecidae) on *Meta* spider (Iwata, 1942). *d,* egg of *Ammophila infesta* (Sphecidae) on noctuid caterpillar (Iwata, 1942). *e,* egg of *Tachysphex costai* (Sphecidae) on an immature *Mantis religiosa* (Grandi, 1961). *f,* egg of *Bembix niponica* (Sphecidae) on a blowfly (Iwata, 1942). *g,* egg of *Pemphredon* (Sphecidae) on an aphid (Iwata, 1942).

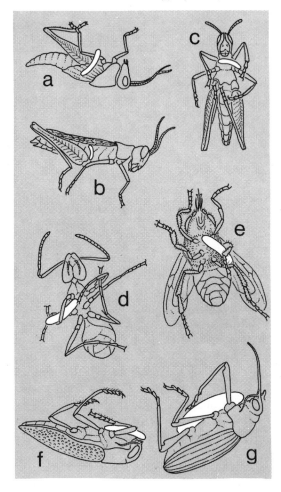

FIG. 16. Eggs of various Sphecidae on prey. *a*, egg of *Stizus fasciatus* on an immature grasshopper (Ferton, 1902). *b*, egg of *Prionyx* on an immature grasshopper (original). *c*, egg of *Tachysphex* on an immature grasshopper (Iwata, 1942). *d*, egg of *Tracheliodes quinquenotatus* on a worker *Tapinoma* ant (Grandi, 1961). *e*, egg of *Philanthus triangulum* on a honeybee (Grandi, 1961). *f*, egg of *Cerceris fumipennis* on a buprestid beetle. *g*, egg of *Cerceris halone* on an acorn weevil. (*f* and *g* original, drawn from photographs).

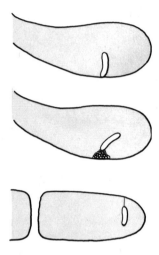

FIG. 17. Eggs of wasps that oviposit in the empty cell, before prey is introduced. Top figure, nest cell of *Microbembex monodonta* (Sphecidae). Middle figure, nest cell of *Bembecinus neglectus* (Sphecidae). Bottom figure, nest cell of *Ancistrocerus antilope* (Eumenidae).

the segmentation of the larva is visible through the very thin wall of the egg. By contractions of the body, over a period of several minutes to an hour or more, the larva releases itself from the egg. K.W. Cooper has observed that in *Ancistrocerus antilope* the hatching larva possesses several clumps of spines on the sides of its body, and these serve as "egg bursters" during the contractions of the body, tearing the wall of the egg and releasing the anterior part of the larva, which immediately begins to feed on the nearest prey. However, the larva remains attached to the shriveled egg shell until undergoing its first molt.

Larval and Pupal Stages

The newly hatched wasp larva often has a rather different appearance from the fully grown larva. Aside from being very much smaller, it is more slender and may be somewhat pointed posteriorly. The head seems disproportionally large, although some of the mouthparts may be incompletely formed. At first the larva feeds on the softer parts of the most available prey in the cell. As it grows it molts several times, five times in *Ancistrocerus antilope* and probably in all wasp larvae, and proceeds to consume all the prey in the cell or presented to it by its mother. In the majority of solitary wasps, the larva does not consume the hard parts of the body of the prey, for example the head capsule, body wall, and wings, and the dismembered hard parts are merely allowed to accumulate in the cell, finally being pushed aside when the cocoon is spun and often coming to cover the outside of the cocoon.

Mature wasp larvae are grublike, usually whitish or cream-colored but sometimes rendered greenish or pinkish if the blood of their prey is of that color (Fig. 18). The head capsule is distinct and may have brownish markings or be wholly brown in color. There are no eyes of any kind, and the antennae are reduced to simple orbits bearing two or three small sensory cones, or these cones may be located at the end of a short or fairly long papilla, resembling a one-segmented antenna. The mandibles or jaws are well developed and provided with powerful muscles which fill much of the head capsule. The maxillae and labium are in the form of fleshy lobes, each bearing conical palpi; the labium also bears a spinneret, which is either in the form of a transverse slit with raised lips or of a pair of sharp projections. The body lacks any evidence of true legs but may have fleshy lobes or pseudopods which assist the larva in making limited movements

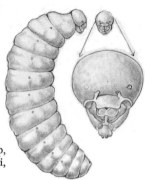

FIG. 18. Larva of a sphecid wasp, *Pemphredon lethifer* (after Grandi, 1961).

within the nest-cell. There are ten pairs of small spiracles. The body wall has a smooth appearance, but under high magnification may be seen to have, in many cases, a covering of minute spines or setae. Most wasp larvae look superficially much alike, but studies have shown that in fact they exhibit considerable diversity in structure, and with sufficient magnification it is usually possible to identify the genus on the basis of structure of the mandibles, maxillae, antennae, spiracles, and so forth.

The fifth-stage larva (after the fourth molt) continues to feed for a period, but soon begins preparations for spinning the cocoon. This generally occurs when the food provided by the mother is exhausted, even though the amount

FIG. 19. Fully-grown larva (left) and cocoon (right) of the digger wasp *Palmodes laeviventris,* a predator on Mormon crickets in western United States. (U.S. Department of Agriculture).

of food may for some reason be smaller than usual; in this case the resulting wasp will be unusually small, or it may fail to reach adulthood. This suggests that cocoon spinning is a simple response to absence of food. But it is not, for if additional food is provided experimentally the larva will often eat some of it, then cease to feed and prepare to spin its cocoon in spite of the presence of additional food. Partially grown larvae which are deprived of food are capable of living for several days and then resuming feeding if food is again available. Under most circumstances, even in cool climates, the larvae of solitary wasps grow very rapidly, and the feeding phase is completed in only a few days—anywhere from three to twelve, but usually about five to seven. Social wasps generally develop more slowly.

Before spinning, the larva cleans the cell by pushing debris to the bottom or the extremities of the cell. Strands of silk, spun from labial glands and discharged through the spinneret, are then attached at various points on the cell wall, forming a loose anchoring framework to which the threads of the cocoon proper are attached. The texture of the cocoon varies greatly in different wasps, depending upon the nature of the silk and the incorporation of other secretions and sometimes soil particles into the cocoon wall. There are also differences in the shape of the cocoon, the presence or absence of a cap, and so forth, so that it is often possible to identify the genus or even the species by the cocoon.

Some digger wasps make exceedingly hard cocoons composed of closely cemented sand grains and lined with layers of silk (Fig. 20). In the sphecid subfamily Nyssoninae, larvae of most species prepare a series of "pores" in the cocoon wall which presumably serve a function in respiration or water exchange. The cocoon-spinning behavior of these insects is exceedingly elaborate, and the entire operation may require as much as two days. In contrast, some twig-nesting wasps make flimsy cocoons or none at all. For example, the common twig-nester *Monobia quad-*

ridens varnishes over the walls of the cell with secretions, but spins no silk. In the social sphecid *Microstigmus comes*, which lives in delicate nests suspended from leaves, the larvae spin no cocoons at all and appear to have no spinnerets. Larvae of the social Vespidae, which develop in elongate cells made of plant material, spin a very thin lining to the cell, but the cell opening is closed with a thick silken cap.

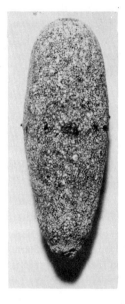

FIG. 20. Cocoon of *Stictia vivida*, a digger wasp that incorporates sand grains into the walls of its cocoon and prepares a series of nipple-like pores around the middle of the cocoon.

Wasp larvae, like those of parasitic Hymenoptera, have no excretory organs; there are no Malpighian tubules and there is no connection between the mid and hind gut. This is a fine adaptation for avoiding contamination of the nest (one which human mothers might envy), but of course these wastes must eventually be eliminated. The fecal material is voided shortly after the cocoon is spun. Surrounded by a delicate membrane, it is discharged into the posterior end of the cocoon as a black mass or "meconium." The urinary wastes, however, remain in the blood as opaque, white globules until the adult stage is reached; only then are the Malpighian tubules formed, permitting the discharge of urinary pellets at the very beginning of adult life.

After defecation within the cocoon, the larva becomes flaccid and enters what is sometimes called the "prepupal stage," although there is no molt at this time and it is still technically a fifth-stage larva. From this point on one of two possible modes of development may be followed. In the case of social Vespidae, or of solitary wasps which are multivoltine—that is, capable of undergoing more than one generation during the summer season—the molt to the pupal stage occurs within a few days, and about two weeks later the adult wasp emerges. In solitary wasps which are univoltine—having but one generation per year —the prepupa remains dormant for many months, and cold temperatures are required to break the diapause (period of dormancy). This also occurs in the final yearly generation of multivoltine species occurring in areas where there is a pronounced winter season. Such wasps pupate in the spring or early summer of the following year and emerge as adults roughly two weeks later.

In the temperate and subarctic zones, the vast majority of wasps overwinter as diapausing larvae or "prepupae" in their cocoons, and even in the tropics many species are active only during certain seasons and at other times undergo diapause as fully fed, resting larvae in their cocoons. Social Vespidae provide a notable exception to this, for few if any have a prolonged larval diapause, and those occurring in cool climates overwinter as fertilized adult females in crevices, under bark, in abandoned mouse nests, and so forth. A very few solitary wasps also overwinter as fertilized females, ready to begin nesting early the following spring. In these cases mating occurs in the fall and the males fail to survive the winter.

Adult Feeding and Maintenance Behavior

Adult wasps require liquid food periodically during their lives, and the major source of nourishment of many species is nectar. Short-tongued wasps, including Tiphiidae, Pompilidae, and many Sphecidae, feed chiefly on Umbelliferae, Euphorbiaceae, and other flowers with shallow corollas, while wasps with more elongate mouthparts

FIG. 21. A female *Isodontia mexicana* (Sphecidae) taking nectar from the blossoms of white sweet clover, *Melilotus*.

(for example *Bembix* and *Ammophila* in the Sphecidae) are able to exploit a great variety of flowers. Members of the sphecid genus *Steniolia* have mouthparts longer than those of most bees, enabling them to exploit the blossoms of legumes and composites in the deserts and dry plains where they occur. Some wasps feed at flowing plant sap, and at least one species is reported to make lesions in plants and feed at the oozing sap. Yellow jackets are much attracted to the juices of ripe fruits, although they generally avail themselves of pre-existing cracks and holes in the fruit and are rarely serious pests of sound fruit. As summer picnickers are all too well aware, yellow jackets are not above sampling jam and lemonade.

Many of the smaller wasps rarely or never visit flowers, and subsist largely on honeydew, the sweet substance produced by aphids and other sucking insects. Females which prey upon flower-feeding insects often obtain liquid carbohydrates by pausing en route to their nest and squeezing out the contents of the prey's crop or food pouch. "Honey robbing" of this nature has been observed, for example, in species of *Philanthus*, which prey upon bees, and in species of *Bembix* employing flower-flies as prey.

Females of some solitary wasps also feed upon the body fluids of their prey, either instead of or in addition to nectar and honeydew. At times this involves simple imbibing of the blood which exudes from the puncture made by the sting. More commonly, the wasp squeezes or chews a portion of the prey with its mandibles and laps up the blood which exudes. This is commonly termed "malaxation." In most cases the prey is later placed in the nest, but in some instances malaxated prey is discarded. For example, spider wasps sometimes capture spiders smaller than nor-

FIG. 22. A male *Polistes* (Vespidae) imbibing watermelon left from a picnic. (Photograph by Richard F. Trump).

mally used for stocking their nest, chew a hole in the abdomen, feed upon the exuding blood, and then leave the spider on the ground. Certain Sphecidae have been reported to capture a series of small prey and feed on them directly rather than using them to stock the nest. Feeding of adult wasps on the prey probably often occurs under conditions of scarcity of nectar or honeydew, but certain species may require proteinaceous food as adults. Social wasps soften their prey by chewing before feeding it to their larvae, and it is probable that they obtain water and nutriments in this way.

Like many other insects, wasps often pause in their activities and clean themselves by rubbing various body parts together. The antennae are passed through the "antennal cleaner" between the front tibial spur and the front tarsus; the eyes and top and sides of the head and thorax are rubbed with the fore legs; the fore legs are cleaned with the mouthparts; the abdomen and wings are cleaned by rubbing the fine brushes on the inner side of the hind legs against them; and the middle and hind legs are rubbed against one another. Even the open tip of the abdomen and its exposed sting apparatus are groomed. These movements apparently serve to free the body of particles of soil, pollen, and other foreign matter, so that these do not interfere with movement, vision, or the chemical senses. When soil-nesting wasps emerge from a bout of digging, for example, they often spend several seconds or even minutes cleaning their body and appendages.

Wasps are decidedly sun-loving animals, and most species are active only when it is warm and there is at least partial sunshine. At night and during inclement weather they remain inactive and are usually said to "sleep," although some persons prefer a less anthropomorphic word such as "akinesis" to describe those periods in which the insects cannot be readily aroused. Wasps sleep either on plants or in their nests. In the former case they assume particular locations and poses, often characteristic of the genus to which they belong, and hold on to the substrate so tightly by means of their mandibles or legs that even a strong wind or rain cannot dislodge them (Fig. 23). Certain plants sometimes attract sleeping wasps and bees in considerable numbers night after night. Such "sleeping bushes" may harbor several species, but each species tends to be localized in one part of the bush and to return to the same perch or perches each evening. The composition of the Hymenoptera present may change each night, suggesting that individuals enter the bush not so much from memory as from some attractive properties of the plant, either its special physical properties or, more probably, as the result of chemical traces left by previous wasps and perhaps also visual cues provided by a few wasps that sleep in the plant regularly.

A few wasps which are solitary ground-nesters form dense and sometimes massive sleeping clusters, all of one species, on plants at some distance from the nesting sites. In some cases the males alone form the clusters, for example in the tiphiid genus *Myzinum* and in some species of the digger wasp genus *Sphex*. In other cases the two sexes

FIG. 23. Two thread-waisted wasps (*Ammophila*) in characteristic sleeping poses on a sweet clover (*Melilotus*).

cluster together, although at certain times one sex may predominate. Clusters of several hundred individuals have been reported in the genera *Zyzzyx* and *Steniolia* (Fig. 24), and clusters "the size of a baby's head" and containing more than a thousand individuals have been reported in the genus *Bembecinus*. The function of these sleeping aggregations remains obscure. There is no evidence that temperature is increased materially inside the clusters or that protection from physical or biotic factors in the environment is increased. Some persons have assumed that these clusters represent an early stage in the origin of sociality, but in fact none of the genera which form sleeping

FIG. 24. A sleeping cluster of *Steniolia obliqua* (Sphecidae) on lodgepole pine. Both males and females are represented in this cluster.

clusters appear to be on the ancestral lines of social species, and the aggregations have no connection with nest building or brood care.

In a number of solitary wasps, the males sleep in vegetation while the females sleep in their nests. In other cases both sexes sleep in the nest, the males often in abandoned nests or other holes. In certain genera (*Philanthus, Bembix*) the males are effective diggers and dig short "sleeping burrows" of their own. In the small digger wasp *Microbembex monodonta* both males and females dig short sleeping burrows; even though the females maintain a brood nest over a period of several days, they spend their inactive periods in separate burrows.

Social wasps generally spend the night in, on, or very near their nest. At the end of the season, in cool climates, the fertilized females hibernate in protected places. Those that survive the winter will found new nests in the spring, often near the site of the old nest, but nothing survives the winter in the nests and they are very seldom used a second year. However, some tropical social wasps have perennial nests, which are occupied and expanded over several years.

Mating Behavior

Male solitary wasps usually emerge several days before the female, a phenomenon called "proterandry" which apparently results from the fact that the pupal stage of the male requires several days less than that of the female. Males of ground-nesters may often be seen flying in great numbers close to the ground in circular or irregular patterns. Such prenuptial flights have sometimes been called "sun dances." Each male tends to patrol a particular area and to pounce upon any insects he encounters, including other males. In some species the males are territorial, taking up perches on or near the ground to which they return repeatedly, and pursuing insects or other flying objects in their vicinity. In the cicada killer, *Sphecius speciosus,* reactions of males to intruders in their territories terminate in one of four ways: (1) unsuccessful pursuit, (2) threat (pursuit broken off within striking distance), (3) butting, and (4) grappling. Grappling occurs only with other *Sphecius* males, especially those in adjacent territories. Male territoriality has also been observed in the digger wasp genera *Astata, Tachytes, Philanthus,* and *Stictia,* and it may be more widespread than now appreciated. Territoriality in these wasps is probably a mechanism for assuring that all emerging females are promptly inseminated.

In the digger wasp genus *Oxybelus,* males of at least one species are known to set up territories at the entrances to active nests and pursue approaching insects, including fly parasites as well as other male *Oxybelus.* When the female arrives at the nest the male copulates with her, sometimes several times in one day. Some species of *Pison* and *Trypoxylon* are unique in that the male remains within the nest when the female is absent, acting as a guard, and mounting the female when she enters the nest; in these wasps the male may participate slightly in nest care, although such behavior is otherwise unknown among wasps.

FIG. 25. A male cicada killer, *Sphecius speciosus,* in a characteristic alert posture on a territorial perch. In this case the perch is the step of a dormitory at Harvard University, overlooking a small nesting aggregation.

In *Oxybelus, Trypoxylon,* and some other genera, the female mates several times over a period of days, but more commonly she mates one or more times soon after emergence and thereafter signals her unwillingness to mate by a characteristic flight or by moving the abdomen or legs in such a way that the male is unable to make contact. In species in which multiple matings occur, the males often live as long as the females, but in the majority of species the males are short-lived, dying after only two or three weeks. In contrast, females commonly live one to two months, or of course much longer if overwintering occurs in the adult stage.

In some cases the male responds to visual cues provided by the female. By using wooden models and dead wasps, G. P. Baerends found that the male *Ammophila pubescens* responds to objects about the size, shape, and color of the female, not necessarily in motion. In many species the colored bands on the female's body may serve as recognition signals, and this may account in part for the many species differences in color pattern. In the tiphiid subfamily Thynninae, the females are reported to assume an immobile "waiting posture" on the ground or the trunks of trees. Here they evidently produce a volatile substance (pheromone) which attracts males of their own species but not of others. There is growing evidence that female wasps of various groups produce such chemical attractants.

The attraction of certain male wasps to the form and odor of the female has been "parasitized" by certain orchids. The blossoms of these plants mimic the female wasps and thus attract males which insure their pollination. For example, males of the European digger wasp *Argogorytes mystaceus* fly to flowers of the orchid *Ophrys insectifera,* which produce an odor resembling the female pheromone; once on the flower, the male is stimulated by the color and shape of the labellum to attempt copulation, and in so doing effects pollination. In Morocco a scoliid wasp is said to bear the same relationship with *Ophrys speculum.*

In most wasps, the male mounts the female from above, straddling her body and holding her with his mandibles or legs, or sometimes both. The initial contact may be in flight, but the pair come to rest on the ground or vegetation, where they remain together anywhere from a few seconds to an hour or more. While the male is astride the female, he may stroke or grasp her antennae with his. During actual copulation, the tip of his abdomen is twisted downward and the genitalia inserted into the bursa copulatrix of the female, the sting being drawn in or moved to one side. Copulation in the social wasp *Polistes* demonstrates this well, and is discussed and illustrated in Chapter IV.

In the digger wasp genus *Ammophila,* the male may remain astride the female for an hour or more, holding on to her with his mandibles, and the pair may fly from flower to flower (Fig. 26); actual copulations are, however, brief, and ten or more may occur during an hour. In some wasps, the male mounts in the usual manner, but after making genitalic contact dismounts and faces in the opposite direction. Mating in the cicada killer, *Sphecius,* is of this type; in this case the pair remains together for forty-five minutes or more and if disturbed may fly about, the larger female carrying the male behind her.

There are several groups of wasps in which the female is wingless and the male carries the female about for an hour or more during mating, suspended from his posterior

FIG. 26. A mating pair of *Ammophila,* the male above the female.

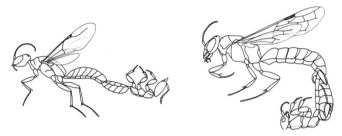

FIG. 27. Phoretic copulation in a bethylid wasp, *Apenesia nitida* (left) and in a tiphiid wasp, *Dimorphothynnus haemorrhoidalis* (right). In each case the male is on the left, the wingless female on the right. Note that in the left figure the female is inverted, while in the right the female is dorsum-up, like the male. (Evans, 1969).

end by the interlocking genitalia. This is the case in certain genera of Bethylidae, Mutillidae, and Tiphiidae. In the tiphiid subfamily Thynninae, the male may carry the female to a feeding site (usually honeydew or extrafloral nectaries), or he may feed her by regurgitation or by a food bolus carried in his specialized mouthparts. Since the females of these wasps are not only wingless but short-legged and sometimes blind or nearly so, "phoretic copulation," as it is called, may play an important role not only in insemination but in dissemination of the species.

Predatory Behavior

It is one of the striking features of wasps that the males show no evidences of predatory behavior, while the females are among the most energetic and efficient predators to be found anywhere in the animal kingdom. As mentioned earlier, instances are known in which the females malaxate and feed upon their prey or squeeze out the crop contents, and apparently in some cases prey is captured primarily for direct feeding. But in the vast majority of cases, the prey is taken directly to the nest, where it serves as food for the larvae.

These remarks do not apply to wasps which are parasites of other wasps or of bees, for example cuckoo wasps (Chrysididae) and "velvet ants" (Mutillidae), groups which we shall examine in Chapter VI. The remarks regarding predation also do not apply to another unusual group, the family Masaridae. A member of one of the more primitive subfamilies is reported to prey on beetle larvae, but most masarids provision their nests with pollen and nectar, in the manner of bees (Fig. 28). Unlike bees, masarid wasps are not very hairy and have no pollen-carrying devices on the legs or abdomen, the female merely carrying the pollen-nectar mixture in her crop or "honey stomach." Many masarids forage on only one or a few genera of plants, and in many cases their mouthparts are specialized for extracting nectar from certain kinds of plants. For example, members of the genus *Pseudomasaris*, of the western United States, re-

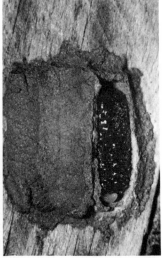

FIG. 28. Left, a female *Pseudomasaris edwardsii* collecting nectar from *Phacelia*. Right, a nest of this species with one cell opened to expose egg of wasp and mass of *Phacelia* pollen and nectar. (Photographs by Philip F. Torchio).

strict their foraging largely to species of *Phacelia, Pent-stemon,* and *Eriodictyon.* Most masarids are not very common insects, and it seems that these wasps were a good deal less successful in exploiting nectar and pollen as larval food than were those Sphecoidea that gave rise to the bees.

One of the most interesting features of predation among solitary wasps is the host-specificity of the majority of species. This can be demonstrated in almost any area of bare, easily crumbled (friable) soil inhabited by ground-nesting species. For example, a small sandpit near the senior author's home in Lexington, Massachusetts, is inhabited by *Bembix spinolae,* a predator on flies, *Ammophila urnaria,* a predator on caterpillars, a species of *Philanthus,* which takes only bees, and three species of *Cerceris,* all preying on beetles, but one taking only leaf beetles of certain species, one acorn weevils (*Curculio*), and one taking only "shining flower beetles" (Phalacridae) which occur in goldenrod blossoms. Each wasp is a specialist in finding, stinging, and handling this particular kind of prey and no other, not only here but throughout its range. By so specializing, wasps effectively "divide up"

FIG. 29. A female digger wasp of the genus *Cerceris* arriving near her nest with a paralyzed weevil. (Photograph by Edward S. Ross).

FIG. 30. A female digger wasp of the genus *Liris* dragging a cricket by its antennae. These wasps take only crickets, just as many species of *Cerceris* take only weevils. (Photograph by Edward S. Ross).

the arthropods available in any one area. Since the arthropods used as prey are generally those present in large numbers during the nesting season, and since each species is a specialist, it is not likely that food shortage is often a limiting factor in wasp abundance.

The adaptation of a particular wasp to its prey presents one of the most intriguing problems in the study of behavior. A few wasps appear (on the basis of present knowledge, at least) to be wholly monophagous—that is, to use a single species as prey. A good example is provided by *Clypeadon laticinctus,* a small digger wasp occurring in the western plains and Rocky Mountains of the United States and specializing on workers of the very common prairie mound-building ant, *Pogonomyrmex occidentalis* (Fig. 44). The *Clypeadon* females fly to the entrances of ant nests, poise rigidly with outstretched antennae, and when a worker ant leaves or tries to enter the nest they pounce upon it quickly and sting it to immediate immobility before the ant is able to use its mandibles or its own powerful sting. If no worker ants are outside of the nest, *Clypeadon* will enter the nest, to emerge a moment later unscathed, often with a paralyzed ant. In Arizona, a related species, *C. haigi,* appears to specialize on *Pogonomyrmex barbatus rugosus* while avoiding another harvester ant occurring in the same situations, *P. maricopa.* The latter species appears to be the normal prey of *Clypeadon sculleni.*

Almost equally strong specialization is shown by a related wasp common in the eastern United States, *Aphilanthops frigidus.* This wasp is a specialist on *Formica fusca* and a few closely related species of ants, but rather than taking workers, it preys only on queens during their nuptial flights, and the active period of the wasp coincides closely with the time of the nuptial flights of these ants. Curiously, the wasps take only queens before they have shed their wings, yet in the nest the wings are removed before the ants are placed in the cell.

Predation on a few related species of the same genus or closely related genera is fairly common; other good examples are provided by the species of *Cerceris* mentioned earlier. This genus holds a special place in the history of entomology, for it was Léon Dufour's essay (1841) on a European *Cerceris* that provisions its nest with metallic wood-boring beetles (Buprestidae) that started Jean Henri Fabre on his career as chronicler of the lives of wasps and many other insects. Dufour marveled at the ability of the wasps to collect great numbers of these brilliantly colored but elusive insects. He collected 450 buprestid beetles from several *Cerceris* nests, remarking as follows:

"You should have heard our exclamations each time that the mine was turned upside down and new glories stood revealed, rendered more brilliant still by the blazing sun; or when we discovered, here, larvae of all ages fastened to their prey, there, the cocoons of those larvae all encrusted with copper, bronze and emerald."

Many persons since Dufour's time have remarked on the ability of wasps to seek out their prey and to collect insects that the entomologist has difficulty in finding, sometimes in the forest canopy or in unusual niches. In 1915 Herbert Lang of the American Museum of Natural History took nearly a thousand flies from females of *Bembix dira* in the Congo. These were found to consist of more than two hundred species belonging to fourteen families. Many of them were described as new, and several had not been rediscovered since.

In *Bembix* and in many other genera, the females prey not upon a few related species but on a broad spectrum of species of one or several families. Some species of *Philanthus* not only take bees of several families but also various wasps and even parasitic Hymenoptera. In a few instances, wasps cross ordinal lines and take quite unrelated insects. For example, the minute digger wasp *Lindenius columbianus* provisions its nest with a mixture of small flies, sucking bugs, and parasitic Hymenoptera. Another unusual wasp is *Microbembex monodonta,* a common inhabitant of beaches and sand dunes all over North America. This wasp stocks its nests with insects of at least ten different orders as well as with spiders, and experimentally it will accept insects of still other orders as well as pieces of centipedes, millipedes, and sowbugs (but not pieces of earthworms or of ham sandwiches!). Only dead or disabled arthropods are used. In other words, this wasp has not only lost all semblance of host-specificity, but it has become a scavenger. One wonders why this mode of life has not become more prevalent among wasps. Perhaps

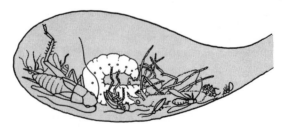

FIG. 31. A larva of *Microbembex monodonta* in the nest cell, feeding on a variety of dead arthropods (drawn from a photograph).

the reason is that the scavenger niche was amply filled at an earlier date by another major group of Hymenoptera, the ants.

The examples cited so far are all digger wasps (Sphecidae), a family which collectively preys upon most kinds of terrestrial arthropods, but in which the various subfamilies, genera, and species show varying degrees of host-specificity. For example, all members of the small subfamily Ampulicinae prey upon cockroaches, but in the related but larger subfamily Sphecinae three types of prey are utilized: Orthoptera (chiefly crickets and grasshoppers, but one genus, *Podium,* on cockroaches), spiders (in two related genera of mud-daubers), and the larvae of Lepidoptera (in the tribe Ammophilini). In this subfamily, as in most others, one notes a correlation between prey type and evolution as deduced from structural characters (Fig. 32). Taking the Sphecidae as a whole, one finds that the groups which are ranked as primitive on structural grounds (such as the Ampulicinae and Sphecinae) for the most part prey on ancient groups of arthropods, while more advanced types of arthropods such as bees and flies are exploited chiefly by structurally more advanced and apparently more recently evolved subfamilies such as the Philanthinae and Nyssoninae (Fig. 33). Apparently as the insects evolved new types, the digger wasps evolved so as to exploit these new sources of food.

The remaining families of predatory wasps stand in contrast to the Sphecidae, for in several cases entire families prey upon one particular type of arthropod and little divergence in prey selection has occurred. So far as known, all members of the large family Pompilidae prey upon spiders, and furthermore use only one spider per nest-cell, so they prey upon spiders approximately their own size. Scoliidae and Tiphiidae are predators on the larvae of beetles occurring in the soil or rotten wood; most of them attack white grubs (Scarabaeidae), but one subfamily of Tiphiidae, the Methochinae, attacks the larvae of tiger beetles (Cicindelidae). Bethylidae restrict their attacks to beetle larvae occurring in the soil or in wood, except that members of one subfamily, the Bethylinae, attack moth larvae occurring in seeds, leaf rolls, stems, and similar situations. Eumenidae prey principally upon caterpillars, although a few of them utilize the caterpillar-like grubs of certain leaf-feeding beetles.

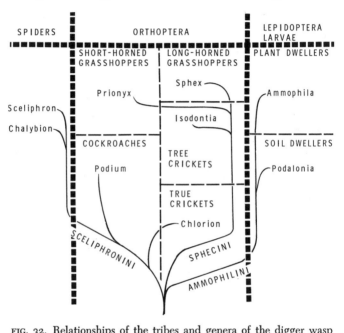

FIG. 32. Relationships of the tribes and genera of the digger wasp subfamily Sphecinae. Although only prey type is indicated here, this arrangement is also supported by adult and larval structure, by type of nest, and by still other features.

Within each of these families, the genera and species exhibit varying degrees of further host-specificity, in some cases involving profound structural modifications. For example, the females of many Bethylidae and Tiphiidae that attack larvae living in the ground or in wood are wingless, and female Pompilidae that attack trap-door spiders have

	SPIDERS	COLLEMBOLA	EPHEMERIDA	ORTHOPTERA	PSOCOPTERA	HEMIPTERA	THYSANOPTERA	LEPIDOPTERA	DIPTERA	COLEOPTERA	HYMENOPTERA
Ampulicinae				X							
Sphecinae	X			X			X				
Pemphredoninae		X				X	X				
Astatinae						X					
Larrinae	X			X		X					X
Crabroninae			X	X	X	X		X	X	X	X
Mellininae									X		
Nyssoninae				X		X		X	X		X
Philanthinae										X	X

FIG. 33. Table showing the subfamilies of digger wasps (Sphecidae), in the left column, and the kinds of arthropods utilized as prey.

the head, clypeus, and fore legs modified so as to aid in penetrating the burrows of their hosts.

The social Vespidae are believed to have evolved from the same stock as the Eumenidae, and as might be expected, many of them prey extensively upon caterpillars. Some of our common paper wasps of the genus *Polistes*, for example, are of importance in the natural control of such insects as the tobacco hornworm. But by and large the social wasps have lost their host-specificity, and attack a variety of arthropods which are common in the vicinity of their nests, often including great numbers of flies, sucking bugs, and so forth. These wasps do not sting their prey, but simply pounce upon it, cut it up with their mandibles, and chew it into a paste. In some cases they will even cut pieces from the flesh of dead vertebrate animals.

Hunting wasps first fly into a habitat suitable for finding prey. Needless to say, species which are highly host-specific tend to seek a more specific niche, for example, the rim of an ant nest (*Clypeadon*) or the limbs of trees harboring cicadas (*Sphecius*). Seeking of the hunting grounds is primarily visual, and a successful hunter may remember the site of prey capture and return again and again for additional prey. This is often reflected in the nest contents of neighboring females in one aggregation. One *Bembix,* for example, may take a series of male horseflies from their perches, while another nesting nearby fills her nest with blowflies taken from a carcass. In the hunting site, the first response to prey is often also visual; a *Bembix* hunting flies at cattle droppings may, for example, dash at a flying dung beetle. However, at close range olfactory cues, as perceived by the antennae, are generally of overriding importance.

It has been shown that *Philanthus* females, deprived of their antennae, are unable to take prey although they can to orient to their nests correctly. N. Tinbergen demonstrated that *Philanthus* females hunt bees by flying from flower to flower and responding to moving images of appropriate size; at this stage they respond only to visual cues, and are not attracted to bees placed out of sight in open tubes. After the wasp approaches the prey downwind at a distance of ten to fifteen centimeters, odor suddenly becomes important, and if the proper stimulus is received, the wasp leaps upon its prey, although stinging occurs only upon reception of additional stimuli, probably of a tactile nature (Fig. 34). Female *Philanthus* will attack dummies of the size and shape of the honeybee if these are shaken with bees to give them the appropriate scent, but only if the dummies are presented at the appropriate stage in the reaction chain.

The importance of the prey's odor explains why hunting wasps are never deceived by visual mimics. Fly predators such as *Bembix,* for example, often use flies which mimic bees and wasps, while bee predators such as *Philanthus* never use drone flies or other flies which mimic bees. There is much evidence that such mimicry is effective primarily with vertebrate predators which rely heavily upon visual cues, especially birds.

In *Philanthus* the female normally stings her prey only once. The sting is inserted in the membrane behind one of the front coxae, and is guided to its target by tactile stimuli received by sense organs on the sting and sting-sheaths (Fig. 35). In contrast, the cricket predator *Liris nigra* normally stings its prey four times, first at the base of the hind (jumping) legs, then at the base of the front legs, middle legs, and finally in the neck membrane.

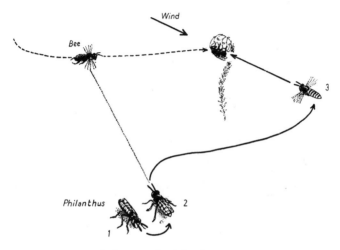

FIG. 34. Hunting behavior of *Philanthus triangulum*. At 2 the wasp is responding to the sight of a bee; she follows the bee and then hovers down-wind from it (at 3), where she responds to the odor of the bee. (N. Tinbergen, 1951).

Again, the insertion of sting is guided by tactile stimuli received by the sting apparatus. Predators on caterpillars and other larvae may sting the prey along the length of the body at quite a number of points.

It was formerly believed that solitary wasps injected venom directly into the nerve ganglia. Recent histological studies have shown that in many cases the sting does not pierce the ganglia or nerve cord. Immobilization starts at the point of puncture and spreads progressively, indicating that paralysis is not produced via the central nervous system but through peripheral blockage. Werner Rathmayer caused *Philanthus triangulum* females to sting honeybees in abnormal places by cutting a window in the integument and placing the sting there. Paralysis was produced merely by introducing venom into the bloodstream; the farther the point of puncture was from the legs and wings, the longer it took for movements to cease (Fig. 36). It seems probable that the number and sequence of stings reflects not the position of the nerve

FIG. 35. Female *Philanthus triangulum* stinging a honeybee. (W. Rathmayer, 1966).

ganglia but the nature of the locomotory system. In bees and flies a single sting in the thorax permits rapid diffusion to the neuromuscular mechanisms of flight and walking; in crickets an initial sting at the base of the jumping legs precedes stings at the base of the other legs; and in caterpillars stings are applied in the vicinity of the abdominal prolegs.

The usual effect of the sting is to place the prey in profound paralysis for a period of several days, after which time it will normally have been consumed by the larva.

However, in many Tiphiidae and Pompilidae and in some Sphecidae the prey recovers partially or completely from the effects of the sting, sometimes within a few hours, although in most cases the prey is packed into the cell in such a way that it cannot escape. In other cases paralysis is long-lasting and seems to have a preservative effect;

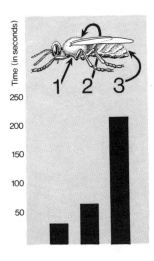

FIG. 36. Histogram showing the amount of time required for the onset of paralysis of a honeybee's legs when venom of *Philanthus* was injected at points 1, 2, and 3. (After W. Rathmayer, 1966).

in one case a spider is said to have lived for four months after being stung by a pompilid. In still other cases the prey dies fairly soon after being stung. This is especially apt to be true in progressive provisioners, that is, wasps which bring in prey day by day as the larva grows rather than merely packing the cell full initially, for in this case the prey is devoured promptly and need not remain fresh for several days. In some species of *Bembix*, the egg is laid on the initial fly but no additional flies are added until the egg hatches two days later; by this time the initial fly, which was killed by the sting, is somewhat stiff and desiccated, and it is not usually eaten by the larva—it has become a mere pedestal for the egg and newly hatched larva.

Little is known about the venom of solitary wasps except that it is evidently very different chemically from that of social wasps. In most cases it is not specific for a

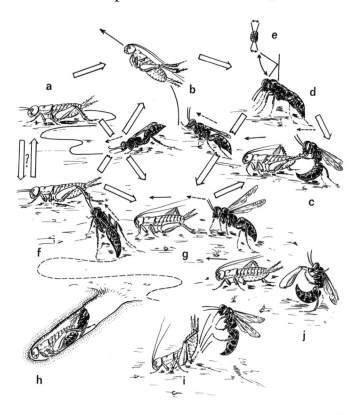

FIG. 37. Interactions of *Liris nigra* with its cricket prey. Broad arrows indicate possible order of phases of behavior, small arrows movements of wasp and prey. At *a*, wasp is tracking prey by scent; at *b*, wasp attacks but prey jumps away; at *c*, wasp seizes a leg and attempts to sting prey. At *d*, pursuit is disrupted and wasp assumes a "head-up" position with side-to-side movements of the body (*e*). At *f*, wasp detects cricket by sight, and at *g* wasp prepares to attack but prey moves away. At *h*, wasp enters cricket's burrow and attacks it there; at *i*, prey defends itself by kicking wasp away; at *j*, cricket loses leg to wasp but escapes. (A.L. Steiner, 1968).

certain type of prey. For example, *Philanthus* venom, when artificially injected into spiders, grasshoppers, and other types of arthropods besides the usual prey, is effective in bringing about paralysis. However, some substance in the blood of *Philanthus* renders it immune to its own venom. *Palarus variegatus,* a wasp that preys upon *Philanthus* and other wasps and bees, is also immune to *Philanthus* venom, although *Philanthus* is not immune to *Palarus* venom. *Palarus* is even known to prey upon social wasps.

Social wasps (Vespidae) no longer use their sting for paralyzing their prey, which is simply seized and chewed into a mass. These wasps have evolved powerful venoms containing several proteinaceous substances which produce severe pain and often systemic effects when injected into vertebrates. The chemistry of the venom is somewhat similar to that of the honeybee and to that of nettle in the plant kingdom, a striking example of the use of similar defensive substances by very different organisms.

Prey Carriage

Once the prey has been subdued, it must be carried to the nest. At first glance this might appear to be a fairly simple process and worthy of little attention. Actually it is one of the more fascinating aspects of the natural history of wasps, for manner of prey carriage is one of the most stereotyped aspects of behavior and in general bears little relationship to the type of prey carried. Prey type and prey carriage have evidently evolved independently of each other, and the two are combined in different ways in different genera. For example, the species of *Mellinus* carry flies to the nest in the mandibles, *Bembix* carry flies with their middle legs, and *Oxybelus* carry flies either with their hind legs or impaled upon their sting. But other wasps use their mandibles to carry a great many kinds of prey, and wasps related to *Bembix* use their middle legs to carry such things as stinkbugs and even butterflies.

Actually it is only in the digger wasps (Sphecidae) that one finds such diversity in manner of prey carriage. In all other families of wasps, the prey is simply seized with the mandibles. Some wasps which utilize one large prey per egg (some Tiphiidae) or a large prey for several eggs (some Bethylidae) may not move the prey at all, but leave it *in situ*. In others, whether or not the prey is moved depends upon the situation. For example, members of the tiphiid genus *Methocha* attack tiger beetle larvae in their vertical burrows in the soil, sting them,

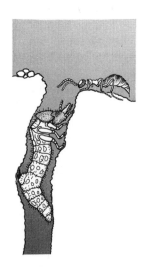

FIG. 38. A female *Methocha* approaching the burrow of its prey, the larva of a tiger beetle. *Methocha* is a tiphiid wasp, although the females are wingless and superficially antlike. (After F.X. Williams, 1919).

lay their egg, and seal off the burrow (Fig. 38). However, if a tiger beetle larva is encountered outside its burrow, it is stung and dragged backward until a suitable hole is found. The prey is generally much heavier than the wasp; the Japanese entomologist Kunio Iwata found a *Methocha* dragging a larva twenty times its own weight.

All spider wasps (Pompilidae) use a single spider per nest-cell, and hence take spiders of about their own size or somewhat larger. The majority of species grasp the base of the spider's legs with their mandibles and proceed backward over the ground (Fig. 39). This type of prey transport is essentially "blind," for the important sense organs of the wasp are pointed away from the direction of travel. Such wasps often deposit the prey on the ground at intervals while they explore the terrain ahead; here it is often subjected to attacks by ants, tiger beetles, or other

FIG. 39. The spider wasp *Anoplius fuscus* with her prey. This wasp drags her prey backward over the ground, holding it by the base of a leg. (Photograph by László Móczár).

predators. It was an important advance when certain spider wasps acquired the ability to hold the spider off the ground and to proceed forward, even though in some cases the prey tended to block the view and to impede walking. Members of the genus *Auplopus* and several related genera characteristically amputate the spider's legs soon after it is stung. They then straddle the spider, seize the spinnerets with their mandibles, and proceed rapidly forward (Fig. 40). This remarkable behavior may have evolved from simple malaxation of the prey, as occurs in many wasps; removal of all of the legs may have been favored by natural selection because it improved the efficiency of prey transport.

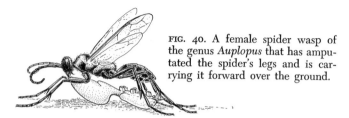

FIG. 40. A female spider wasp of the genus *Auplopus* that has amputated the spider's legs and is carrying it forward over the ground.

The pompilid *Anoplius depressipes,* which preys upon aquatic spiders of the genus *Dolomedes* and nests along watercourses, has been observed flying over the water towing its prey over the surface film. Other spider wasps carry their prey up a stem and take flight from there, while others take flight readily from the ground with spiders weighing little more than themselves, although dragging larger spiders over the ground. However, few if any Pompilidae have proceeded to full and consistent aerial prey transport.

Virtually all members of the family Sphecidae proceed forward with their prey. In this family there has been evolution toward the utilization of smaller prey, several to many of which are used per nest-cell, and such prey is usually carried in flight. However, some of the more generalized genera of this family use a single large prey per nest and proceed over the ground. Members of the genus *Prionyx,* for example, prey upon large grasshoppers and have even been noted following behind swarms of migratory locusts. The grasshoppers are dragged forward to the nest, assisted by rapid movements of the wings which rarely if ever succeed in lifting the prey off the ground; the wasp straddles the prey, holding its antennae between the mandibles and a small notch on the anterior margin of the clypeus. In the related genus *Ammophila,* some species use one or two large caterpillars per nest and carry the prey over the ground, while others use several smaller caterpillars per nest and invariably carry it in flight.

All Eumenidae prey on small caterpillars or beetle larvae and carry the prey forward in flight, holding it with the mandibles and often also embracing it with the legs. Vespidae macerate their prey and carry it in a ball in their mandibles, often assisted by the front legs.

In general, then, we may distinguish three kinds of mandibular prey carriage: (1) backward on the ground, (2) forward on the ground, and (3) forward in flight. In the last two cases, the legs may also support the prey or food mass, but the major grasp is with the mandibles. Since in every case the prey is held far forward, blocking the major digging organs (the mandibles and front legs), these wasps must either (1) leave the nest entrance open so that it may be entered directly upon returning with prey, or (2) deposit the prey at the nest entrance while the closure is removed (Fig. 41). In the first case, the nest may be readily entered by various parasites while the wasp is away—bombyliid flies, for example, deposit their eggs in open holes, and their larvae develop as parasites of wasp larvae. In the second case, the prey is subject to attack by ants or tiger beetles, or may even be stolen by another digger wasp. Females of *Microbembex monodonta* have been observed taking grasshoppers from the nest entrances of *Tachysphex* and caterpillars from the nest entrances of *Ammophila*—two genera in which most species close the nest and must deposit the prey upon re-entering.

It is thus not surprising that in the Sphecidae (but in that family alone!) at least four different stocks have evolved behavior which permits them to re-enter the closed nest without putting down their prey. The most common method involves holding the prey close beneath the center of the body with the middle legs (Fig. 42). Here the prey provides minimum disturbance to the equilibrium of the wasp and is also shielded from attacks by "satellite flies" (*Senotainia*) which larviposit on prey before it is placed in the nest. Most important, the digging

FIG. 41. Four steps in provisioning the nest in *Tachysphex termi-natus* (Sphecidae). At the top, a female approaches her closed nest entrance carrying a grasshopper, holding its antennae in her mandibles. She then deposits the prey, scrapes open the entrance with her front legs and enters, then comes out (lower figure) and draws in the prey. (Photographs by F.E. Kurczewski and N.F.R. Snyder).

of the wasp is unimpaired; when it lands at the nest entrance it can scrape open the entrance with the front legs, assisted by the mandibles if necessary, while standing on the hind legs and holding the prey with the middle legs. Large prey may also be supported loosely by the other legs in flight, but the major grip—and the only grip after landing—is provided by the middle legs. As the wasp enters the burrow, the prey is allowed to slip backward so that it follows the wasp down the small bore of the tunnel; at this time the prey is released by the middle legs and grasped by the hind legs.

FIG. 42. A female *Bembix rostrata* opening the burrow with her front legs while holding her prey (a horsefly) with her middle legs. (Photograph by László Móczár).

Wasps which carry their prey in this manner often range widely in their search for prey and are able to return swiftly to a well concealed nest and to enter quickly and without releasing their prey. Several of the larger and more successful genera of Sphecidae employ this method of prey carriage: *Philanthus* (predators on bees), *Bembix* (flies), *Gorytes* (leafhoppers), *Bicyrtes* (stinkbugs), *Crabro* (flies), and others. The cicada killers (*Sphecius*) carry their very large prey in the same manner, but have special modifications of their hind legs which evidently assist in holding the cicada while in flight.

A few wasps, chiefly of the genus *Oxybelus*, carry their prey farther back beneath the body, holding it with their hind legs. Such wasps are able to avoid a transfer in grasp upon entering the nest and presumably attain an even greater speed of provisioning. It is in this same genus, *Oxybelus*, that we find numerous species which have abandoned pedal in favor of abdominal prey carriage (Fig. 43). In these species the prey is held in about the same position, ventrally near the end of the abdomen, but it is held by the sting, which is weakly barbed. After stinging, these wasps evidently drive the sting into the thorax of the fly, where it remains fastened with no support from the legs. Thus when the wasp lands at the nest entrance it is able to move about and open the nest with all three pairs of legs free.

Still another method of prey carriage on the abdomen occurs in the genus *Clypeadon*. Members of this genus prey upon worker ants of the genus *Pogonomyrmex*, which they capture at the nest entrances and carry swiftly to their own nests suspended from the tips of their abdomens in a head-down position (Fig. 44). In this instance the sting does not appear to play an important role in holding the prey, but the apical abdominal segment is enlarged and specialized. The upper surface is biconcave, fitting against one pair of coxae of the ant, and may have projections which fit against certain structures on the ant; the lower surface is also bilobed and variously modified (Fig. 45, lower figure). Evidently this "ant-clamp" is forced between two pairs of the ant's coxae and slightly spread by muscular action or blood pressure so as to obtain a firm purchase on the ant during flight to the nest. These wasps are able to provision very rapidly and have never been observed to drop their prey.

Curiously, members of the genus *Clypeadon* are relatively uncommon in spite of the fact that the ants they

FIG. 43. Prey carriage in the digger wasp *Oxybelus bipunctatus* (from motion-picture film). At the left, the wasp has arrived at the nest with a fly impaled upon her sting. As she digs into the burrow (right) she assumes a more nearly vertical pose before plunging in.

FIG. 44. A female *Clypeadon laticinctus* digging into her nest entrance while holding a worker harvester ant on the end of her abdomen.

prey upon are exceedingly abundant. Observations indicate that wasps of this genus are very heavily parasitized, particularly by *Senotainia* flies, which larviposit on the prey during transit to the nest. In this particular instance, evolution of a more efficient prey-carrying mechanism may have "backfired," for the ant prey suspended from the tip of the abdomen appears unduly exposed to the attacks of these flies.

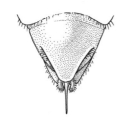

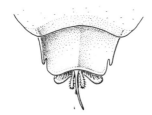

FIG. 45. Apical abdominal segment of a typical digger wasp, *Aphilanthops frigidus* (top), compared to that of *Clypeadon laticinctus* (lower), a species in which it is biconcave and otherwise modified for holding onto its ant prey.

In general, we may characterize prey carriage in wasps as having undergone an evolution independent of prey selection, an evolution molded largely by parasite pressure and by the advantages of foraging widely from the nest and still returning swiftly to it. This evolution has been strongly influenced by the tendency for more advanced wasps to use several small prey per cell rather than one large one, for in general only prey smaller and lighter than the wasp can be carried by the more advanced mechanisms. Starting from a position in front of the head of the wasp, where it effectively blocked the major sense organs and digging mechanisms, the prey was moved ventrally and backward, first to a position near the center of the body (in many genera), then to the end of the abdomen (in a very few genera). Here it is held by the sting itself (*Oxybelus*) or by special modifications of the tip of the abdomen (*Clypeadon*). The fact that only a few wasps employ abdominal prey carriage may reflect the fact that prey suspended from the end of the wasp's body is greatly exposed to attacks by satellite flies; such attacks may effectively cancel out the advantages of having all three pairs of legs free.

Orientation

As might be deduced from these considerations, wasps which forage far from the nest and yet return swiftly to a closed and thoroughly concealed nest entrance must have exceedingly refined powers of orientation. Such wasps often find their nests successfully even after extensive disturbances to landmarks and to the soil surface. Yet in other wasps even minor changes may cause serious disorientation. Evidently wasps orientate principally by visual cues; observation and experiment suggest that odors play little or no role in nest-finding. However, wasps which parasitize other wasps often do appear to employ odor cues in finding the nests of their hosts (see Chapter VI).

In predatory wasps which do not prepare a nest there is, of course, no orientation other than that to the prey. Wasps which dig a simple nest *after* taking prey (many Pompilidae) often deposit the prey in a crevice or in the crotch of a plant while digging (Fig. 46); such wasps often go back and forth between prey and nest several times, sometimes taking considerable time and showing much searching behavior. Wasps which prepare a nest first and return repeatedly to it with prey, however, generally return much more directly. The capacity to learn the location of landmarks with reference to the entrance is doubtless a prerequisite for this mode of life. Such wasps make one or more "orientation flights" or "locality studies" during or after construction of the nest. The cues learned at this time, often in a matter of a few seconds, guide them to the nest on their "homing" or "recognition" flights. Disturbance to landmarks which causes a delay to a returning wasp often results in a "reorientation" flight upon leaving. Needless to say, when a wasp makes the final closure of one nest and digs another, it "forgets" the previous nest location and learns a new one. This is

FIG. 46. A female spider wasp, *Episyron quinquenotatus*, that has suspended her prey from the crotch of a plant while she leaves to dig a nest nearby.

particularly impressive in certain species of *Ammophila* which (alone among well-studied wasps) maintain several active nests at once, yet remember the location of each and "forget" each nest as it is completed.

The nature of the landmarks employed depends very much on the habitat and general behavior of the wasp. Some species of *Ammophila* make orientation flights, yet return over the ground with their heavy prey, so that they see these landmarks in different perspective. They may, however, occasionally leave their prey and fly up a short distance or climb to the top of a plant, evidently to "take sight" on certain landmarks. G. P. Baerends found that female *Ammophila pubescens* learn details of the terrain for some forty meters around the nest and can generally find the nest from anywhere within that distance. This species often uses rows of trees or bushes as cues, and when Baerends prepared artificial trees and moved them about he was able to guide females to incorrect situations at will. Such things as paths, furrows, and rocks are often used as landmarks by *Ammophila,* larger landmarks and patterns being used at some distance from the nest, smaller objects in the immediate vicinity of the nest. Although all species of *Ammophila* close and conceal their nest, many other wasps do not, and in this case the image of the hole and surrounding rim of soil is important (e.g., in *Cerceris*).

Philanthus triangulum, a species studied by N. Tinbergen and his colleagues in Holland, leaves a small mound of earth at the nest entrance which undoubtedly aids the wasp in finding the exact position of the hole. However, other objects in the vicinity, particularly ones having a broken outline and extending well above the sand surface, serve as markers in nest-finding. Tinbergen placed a ring of fir cones around a nest while the wasp was inside, then moved it to one side after she left. The returning wasp flew to the center of the ring of cones and thus failed to find the nest entrance (Fig. 47). In another

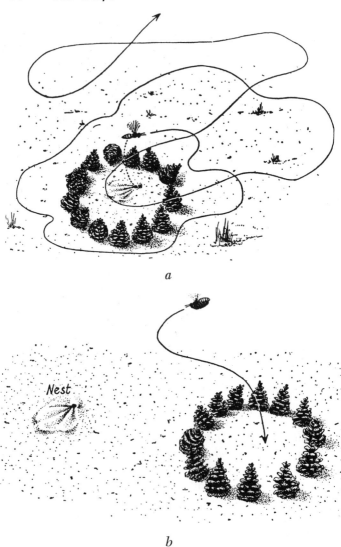

a

b

FIG. 47. *a*, Locality study by a female *Philanthus triangulum* following completion of a nest. *b*, When the ring of cones is displaced to one side, the wasp proceeds to the center of the ring. (N. Tinbergen, 1951).

experiment, Tinbergen placed a ring of alternating black discs and hemispheres around a nest, then while the wasp was away placed the discs in a circle on one side, the hemispheres in a circle on the other side. Returning wasps almost invariably orientated to the hemispheres rather than the flat discs, demonstrating their preference for objects extending above the surface. When given a choice between a solid black ring and a checkered one, they choose the latter, demonstrating a preference for broken patterns. They also learn the relative position of various landmarks. One wasp returned regularly to a nest located near one corner of a square board which faced a branch pushed into the ground some distance away. When board and branch were moved to one side and the board was turned so that its *side* faced the nest, the wasp appeared confused, but searched in the two corners closest to the branch. If the branch was moved opposite one corner, the wasp showed a preference for that corner (Fig. 48). Thus the response was not to an individual landmark, but to a configuration or *gestalt*.

It is convenient to recognize three successive stages in orientation: (1) distant orientation, or departure in the correct direction from a distant hunting site; (2) proximate orientation, or recognition of the nest surroundings; and (3) immediate orientation, or finding of the burrow itself. The outer limits of distant orientation vary greatly, depending upon the hunting behavior and type of prey carriage of the wasp; although only about forty meters in *Ammophila pubescens,* the distance may be as much as a kilometer in some species of *Philanthus* and *Bembix.* Phil Rau carried a marked female mud-dauber (*Sceliphron*) one-third of a mile from her nest, and she returned in twenty-five minutes; a queen paper wasp (*Polistes*) returned to her nest from a distance of two miles, but she took twenty-two hours to do so. There is good reason to believe that flights to and from distant sites involve use of the "sun compass," as in many other insects. That is, the wasp learns the position of the sun in relation to its line of flight, then maintains this same angle in reverse on the return flight. Major configurations of landmarks may also be of great importance in distant orientation, as lesser ones obviously are in proximate orientation, although it is much more difficult to design experiments to test this.

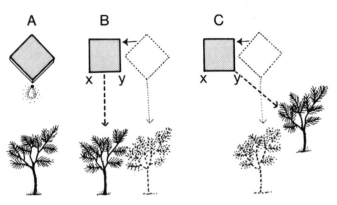

FIG.   48. Nest-finding by *Philanthus triangulum*. At (A), a square board is placed behind a nest entrance and a branch placed in front of it some distance away. After two days, during which the wasp learned to accept these landmarks, branch and board are displaced slightly to the left, the board turned 45 degrees (B); in this instance the returning wasp searches at both *x* and *y*, and sometimes in between. When the branch is displaced so that it is opposite one corner (C), the wasp searches primarily in the nearest corner (*y*). (After G. Van Beusekom, 1948).

Wasps which nest in large colonies in broad expanses of bare sand largely devoid of landmarks would seem to be confronted with major problems in nest-finding, yet such wasps generally find their nests with little difficulty. It appears that sand-loving wasps such as *Bembix* utilize markers without respect to their height but only with respect to their surface area; furthermore, such wasps employ concentric girdles of landmarks, some of which effectively guide them to the nest even when others are severely disturbed. There is evidence that the profile of the horizon, as seen from a position facing the nest, may be of major importance. The Dutch biologist J. van Iersel placed vertical barriers in back of *Bembix* nests and found that these delayed the wasps in finding their nests—except if he placed a window in the barrier revealing the profile of distant hills and trees (Fig. 49).

FIG. 49. Use of distant orientation cues in *Bembex rostrata.* When a large vertical sheet is placed 60 centimeters in front of the nest (left figure), the returning wasp spends much time searching for her nest. But when a window is placed in the sheet, revealing a distant horizon, the wasp often finds the nest immediately. (After J.J.A. van Iersel, 1965).

Although most studies of orientation have been conducted on ground-nesting wasps, there is every reason to suppose that the same principles apply to species nesting in hollow twigs or in aerial nests of mud or paper. We have yet to consider the building of nests and the activities which go on inside them. In the next chapter we shall describe the nesting behavior of solitary wasps, saving the social wasps for the two chapters that follow.

III. *The Nesting Behavior of Solitary Wasps*

The higher Hymenoptera (wasps, ants, and bees) are among the few insects that maintain a nest, which in most cases has become the focal point in their activities. The presence of a nest has undoubtedly been an important predaptation for social life. The nesting behavior of solitary species is also of much intrinsic interest, for nest building and maintenance involve some of the most elaborate and stereotyped behavior patterns. The nests of wasps are of many kinds, and an elaborate terminology has been developed to describe the various forms. We shall avoid most of these terms and use a rather simple classification of nest types (page 76), without pretending that the nest of every species will fit neatly into this classification. Each type of nest in our outline is variable and could readily be broken down into further subtypes. For example, multicellular terrestrial nests (III: C1 in our outline) assume many different forms: the burrow may be vertical or oblique, the mound of soil at the entrance may be left intact or removed in one of various ways, the first cell may be deep in the ground and others built progressively back toward the entrance, or the reverse may be true, and so forth. In those species which use foreign materials in their nests (II: C and IV) the materials used are exceedingly diverse and may be combined in various ways. Nests provide an interesting subject by themselves, for they are in a sense "crystallized behavior"—in the case of social insects, the behavior not of one but of many closely coordinated individuals.

In the broad view, we may say that the most generalized wasps, like their parasitoid ancestors, make no nests at all; somewhat more advanced wasps drag the prey into a crevice or pre-existing hole, which is then closed over; and still more advanced wasps dig nests in the soil, at first very simple in structure but later complex and multicellular. By far the majority of wasps are associated with the soil; this includes virtually all of the Scolioidea, most of the Bethylidae, Pompilidae, and Sphecidae, and some of the Eumenidae and Masaridae. Yet there are diverse elements in the last four of these groups which have taken to life above ground, either by digging in pith or rotten wood, by taking over hollow twigs or borings in wood, or by making nests of mud. Some Eumenidae incorporate macerated wood fibers into their mud nests, and it is apparently from antecedents such as these that the Vespidae evolved their carton nests. Most Vespidae make elaborate aerial nests, but a few (our common ground-nesting yellow jackets) build their paper nests in cavities in the soil.

Although there appears to be a general evolutionary progression from no nests at all to simple and then more complex nests, there have been reversals in these trends as well as many instances of convergence—that is, examples of unrelated wasps making similar nests. The major reversals involve wasps which we know from structural evidence must once have made nests but now seek out, enter, and lay their eggs in the nest-cells of other wasps, their larvae developing on the prey in the nest (I:B) or as parasites of the wasp larvae (I:C). We shall discuss these insects further in Chapter VI. There is good evidence that some species which now make unicellular nests (III:A) are derived from stocks which made multicellular nests (III:B), and even some less conclusive evidence that certain aerial nesters have returned to the ground. It should be noted, incidentally, that ground-

THE KINDS OF NESTS MADE BY WASPS

I. No nest constructed
    A. Prey left *in situ* (Dryinidae, many Bethylidae, Tiphiidae)
    B. Nest and prey of another wasp taken over (cleptoparasitic Pompilidae and Sphecidae)
    C. Develop as parasites of larvae of wasps and bees in their nests (Mutillidae, Chrysididae, Sapygidae)

II. Nest is a pre-existing cavity (often modified)
    A. Prey dragged into its own burrow in soil (usually sealed over) (some Tiphiidae, Pompilidae)
    B. Prey taken to a crevice in or above ground, the crevice then sealed off (many Bethylidae, some Pompilidae)
    C. Cells constructed in hollow twigs or borings, in series separated by partitions
        (1) Partitions of dry soil particles, detritus, plant materials (some Pompilidae, Sphecidae)
        (2) Partitions primarily of mud (Eumenidae, some Sphecidae)

III. Nests dug in ground, rotten wood, or pith of plants
    A. Cells constructed at ends of short burrows from walls of a pre-existing burrow in soil (some Pompilidae, Sphecidae)
    B. Simple, unicellular nests in ground (many Pompilidae, some Sphecidae)
    C. Multicellular nests in soil, rotten wood, or pith
        (1) Cells constructed from main burrow or side-burrows, clustered or widely spaced (many Sphecidae, some Eumenidae)
        (2) Cells in series, separated by partitions (some Sphecidae, Eumenidae)
    D. Multicellular nests in ground having mud entrance turrets (some Eumenidae, Masaridae)

IV. Nests constructed wholly of foreign materials (usually aerial)
    A. Nests primarily of mud
        (1) Cells in a spherical or irregular cluster (some Eumenidae, Sphecidae)
        (2) Cells in parallel mud tubes (some *Trypoxylon* in Sphecidae, *Stenogaster* in Vespidae)
        (3) Separate but adjacent mud cells (some Pompilidae, Eumenidae, some Stenogastrinae in Vespidae)

(4) Tiers of hexagonal cells surrounded by envelope (*Polybia fasciata* in Polistinae, Vespidae)

B. Nests primarily of wood pulp or other plant materials

(1) Spherical cells in irregular cluster in ball of plant fibers suspended by a filament (*Microstigmus* in Sphecidae)

(2) More or less tubular cells in irregular cluster, or in series along plant stem or rootlet (*Parischnogaster* in Stenogastrinae, Vespidae)

(3) Naked paper comb suspended by pedicel(s), or stem(s) (Vespidae: Polistinae such as *Polistes, Mischocyttarus, Apoica*)

(4) More than one naked comb connected by pedicels (*Gymnopolybia* in Vespidae, Polistinae)

(5) Paper comb(s) surrounded by envelope, with comb(s) (Vespidae):

   a. in horizontal tiers connected by pedicels (*Vespula, Charterginus*)

   b. in horizontal tiers connected to sides of envelope (*Polybia, Brachygastra*)

   c. attached directly to substrate (*Metapolybia, Synoeca*)

   d. concentric vertical cylinders (*Stelopolybia argentata*)

   e. spherical (*Stelopolybia meridionalis*)

   f. vertical tiers, attached to envelope by pedicels (*Polybioides, Parachartergus*)

nesters are largely confined to places where the soil is more or less bare and friable. Aerial nesters are not so confined, and are able to nest in a wide variety of situations not open to ground-nesters. In general, ground nesters tend to be most numerous in deserts, plains, dunes, beaches, sandbanks, and artificial excavations, while aerial nesters tend to thrive in wooded or bushy areas. The abundance of wasps in all temperate and tropical regions is a tribute to their evolutionary versatility.

Digging Behavior of Fossorial Wasps

Since so many wasps are associated with the soil, it is logical to discuss fossorial or digging species first and at greatest length. As compared to aerial nesters, ground-nesters tend to have more spines on the legs and often have broader mandibles as well as a well developed, flat pygidial plate (apical abdominal tergite) which is used for tapping or pushing soil. These are the three major digging organs: the mandibles, the legs, and the pygidium. The mandibles are often employed for breaking soil, and tend to be most robust in species that dig in compacted earth (as opposed to sand); the mandibles are also used for dragging pebbles or other objects from the burrow and sometimes for placing objects over the closed nest entrance. Many female Scolioidea spend much time digging in the soil in search of their white grub prey; these insects have short, thick legs which bear many spines and hairs, and they move through the soil by breaking it with their mandibles and pushing it beneath and behind them by thrusts of all three pairs of legs. In the majority of fossorial wasps, however, the middle and hind legs play no important role in digging. Most Pompilidae and Sphecidae which dig in the soil have a series of stout spines on the front tarsus, resembling the teeth of a comb; this is often spoken of as a "tarsal comb," or pecten. Actually it would be more appropriate to call it a rake, since when the tarsi are bent toward the midline of the body and moved rapidly backward and forward, the effect is that of a rake (Figs. 13, 50).

The actual digging of a nest is often preceded by short periods of "trial digging." That is, the wasp digs for a few moments here and there, apparently seeking a location where the soil is sufficiently friable yet not so loose as to permit cave-ins. The precise stimuli which release full nest-digging behavior are not known, and undoubtedly differ from species to species. Some wasps have been observed to dig many incomplete burrows before finally finishing a nest, and some have even been observed to close up these holes before abandoning them. The con-

FIG. 50. *Bembix amoena* (Sphecidae) digging its burrow (above) and closing the burrow entrance (below). Note the series of large spines on the front legs, making up the "tarsal rake."

struction of such abortive burrows may be associated with insufficient "drive"; over a period of time there may be an increase in motivation, so that a proper combination of stimuli releases full nesting behavior. Once the nest is started, the soil may be removed in any of several ways, for which convenient vernacular terms have

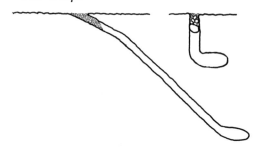

FIG. 51. Two typical unicellular ground nests of Sphecidae. Left, a nest of *Bembix amoena;* right, the short, vertical nest of *Ammophila azteca.* The first is closed with loose sand scraped in the entrance, the second with a plug consisting of a pebble above which smaller pebbles and some loose sand have been placed.

been proposed by the German authority Günter Olberg. He speaks of digger wasps as being either "rakers," "pullers," "pushers," or "carriers." We shall consider these four modes of digging separately.

The "rakers" constitute the majority of fossorial wasps, and most such wasps have the pecten of the front tarsus strongly developed. In most Pompilidae and in some Sphecidae the two front legs move alternately and the abdomen is held high, permitting a more or less continuous stream of soil particles to pass beneath and behind the

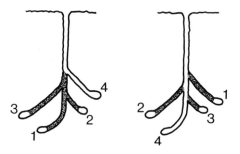

FIG. 52. Two major types of multicellular nests in digger wasps. On the left, the initial cell is deepest and additional cells constructed from side-burrows back toward the entrance; on the right, the initial cell is closest to the entrance, and additional cells are added by deepening the burrow. (After E. T. Nielsen, 1933).

body. In the more advanced digger wasps (*Bembix* is a good example) the two front legs work synchronously, and with each backstroke the abdomen is elevated to accommodate the passage of a jet of soil particles. In such wasps the body undergoes a series of very rapid tilting movements: head and forelimbs down (backstroke) and abdomen up—head up (forelimbs thrust forward) and abdomen down—and so forth. Some digger wasps are able to throw the soil beneath them to a considerable distance (six inches or more) and by turning the body from side to side are able to spray sand from the nest entrance over a considerable area, so that it does not accumulate in a pile at the entrance. However, in most cases such a mound of soil does accumulate, and in many species it is dispersed by special "leveling" movements following completion of the burrow; these movements vary in pattern but most commonly consist of repeated passages over the mound while scraping sand and turning slightly from side to side.

During the actual digging of the burrow, much use is made of the mandibles in breaking soil, as mentioned earlier, and the cylindrical bore is insured by twisting movements within the burrow. Loosened soil is moved up and out of the burrow in a series of steps. Wasps which prepare a series of cells from one burrow often use the soil from the new cell to close off the completed cell and a short section of burrow leading to it. Wasps that prepare complex, many-celled nests, such as many species of *Philanthus,* often do much digging and filling deep in the ground, and are rarely seen digging at the nest entrance after completion of the initial burrow. Virtually all rakers make oblique burrows, since this method of digging is not adaptive for vertical burrows.

"Pullers" resemble rakers in that the burrow is usually oblique and the soil removed with the mouthparts and front legs. However, these structures are used in a very different way. The soil is gathered into a lump which is held between the head and front legs, and the wasp backs out and deposits the lump a short distance from the entrance. Good examples are to be found in the genus *Mellinus* and in the small wasp *Tachytes mergus*. The latter species backs several inches from the entrance and deposits its lump of soil, carrying successive lumps in different directions and leaving a semicircular ridge of pellets. This type of digging behavior is most effective in soils having particles which adhere in clumps, and does not work in dry sand. Certain species have been observed to act as rakers when digging through dry surface sand and to pull out the soil in lumps after reaching moister layers beneath; a good example is provided by the great golden digger, *Sphex ichneumoneus* (Fig. 53).

Digger wasps classified as "pushers" simply back up the burrow pushing soil behind them, often using the front legs or all the legs to move soil, and also using the abdomen as a ram to push the plug of soil along (Olberg compares them to a piston pump). Many such wasps have an especially strong pygidial plate at the end of the abdomen, for example the species of *Cerceris* and *Tachytes*. Members of both of these genera make vertical or near-vertical burrows and simply push the soil into a heap at the entrance; they then make an entrance hole in the center of the mound, which is left as a surrounding rim as in many ants and fossorial bees. The cicada-killer (*Sphecius*) is a pusher of an unusual sort, since it uses the hind legs in a somewhat scissorslike manner to push the soil along as it backs from its oblique burrow. *Sphecius,* like some other pushers, also employs scraping movements in some phases of its nesting behavior. Wasps which mine in rotten wood or the pith of plants are often also pushers, although the burrow may be vertical, oblique, or horizontal depending upon circumstances; such wasps often have a narrow, concave pygidial plate which apparently serves as a scoop for soft wood particles (e.g. in the genus *Ectemnius*).

FIG. 53. The great golden digger, *Sphex ichneumoneus*. Above, a female digging by "pulling" a lump of soil from the burrow; below, the same female returning somewhat later with an immature katydid as prey. (Photographs by Richard F. Trump).

"Carriers" are distinctive in that the soil is actually taken some distance from the nest entrance and deposited, leaving no evidences of digging in the immediate vicinity of the nest. Carriers are perhaps best thought of as highly efficient pullers, since like pullers they hold the soil a lump between the head and front legs. After leaving the nest, they either walk forward away from the entrance and drop the soil (e.g., some species of *Ammophila*) or more commonly fly off and drop it (other species of *Ammophila*, also many ground nesting Vespoidea, including the common ground-nesting yellow jackets). Members of the sphecid genus *Belomicrus,* and

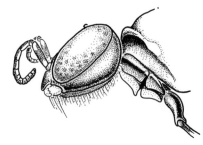

FIG. 54. The psammophore of *Belomicrus forbesii* (Sphecidae), used in carrying a pellet of earth between the head and the thorax.

some other genera, fly swiftly backward from the entrance and drop the soil, then dart quickly back into the burrow to repeat the performance. In these wasps the posterior surface of the head often bears a fringe of long hairs, called a psammophore, which assists in holding the pellet of earth (Fig. 54). In the eumenid genus *Pterocheilus* the palpi are long, flattened, and fringed with setae, apparently serving a similar function (Fig. 55). Eumenids often carry water to the nesting site, using it to soften the earth

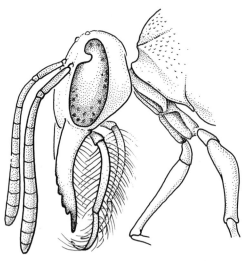

FIG. 55. The fringed palpi and mandibles of *Pterocheilus* (Eumenidae), which form a basket for carrying earth during nest construction.

prior to digging, then carry away the moistened pellet of earth.

The four types of digging behavior reviewed above are not mutually exclusive, for some wasps employ more than one manner of digging or modes of digging somewhat intermediate between the major types. *Ammophila,* for example, often does a certain amount of scraping, especially during nest closure, although it is usually a "carrier." Scraping and pushing, and combinations thereof, are characteristic of more generalized digger wasps; pulling probably evolved as a mechanism for handling more compacted soil, and carrying as a modification of this involving total removal of the soil particles and hence resulting in greater concealment of the nest.

Manner of nest closure is also related to digging behavior. Most rakers close the nest by facing away from the burrow and scraping soil into it (i.e., "digging in reverse"), while some carriers pick up particles and carry them to the nest as fill for the burrow. This behavior is particularly marked in certain species of *Ammophila* in which the females search about for a pebble or pellet of proper size to close the bore of the short, vertical burrow; sometimes several such objects are tried for size and rejected before a suitable one is found (Fig. 56). Such objects as acorns or rabbit pellets have been observed to be used for temporary closure of *Ammophila* burrows. At the time of final closure, the major pellet is placed deep in the burrow and additional, smaller objects are placed above it. Sometimes these pellets are pulverized with blows of the head, and on some occasions the female uses a pebble in the manner of a hammer to pound the fill into a compact plug (Fig. 57). This behavior has been called "intelligent" by some persons, since it involves the use of a simple tool. However, it is a fixed part of the instinctive behavior of several species of *Ammophila,* probably having evolved from carrying behavior combined with pounding movements of the front of the head (which occur in

FIG. 56. A female *Ammophila pubescens* returning to the nest with a pebble that she has selected to fit the bore of the burrow. (Günter Olberg, 1959).

most members of the subfamily Sphecinae, to which *Ammophila* belongs). The wasp, in effect, begins pounding movements before completion of carrying, i.e., before releasing the pebble. This evidently proved a valuable adaptation in those species of *Ammophila* which make vertical burrows in compact soil. "Tool-using" behavior of this nature is absent in members of the genus which nest in friable sand, e.g., in *Ammophila harti*.

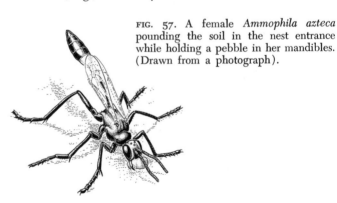

FIG. 57. A female *Ammophila azteca* pounding the soil in the nest entrance while holding a pebble in her mandibles. (Drawn from a photograph).

Although Sphecinae employ the front of the head for pressing soil into the burrow during closure, other Sphecidae and most Pompilidae use the tip of the abdomen rather than the head. The abdomen is twisted downward so that the pygidium is applied to the soil in a series of rapid blows. In certain spider wasps (e.g., *Poecilopompilus interruptus*) these pounding movements with the tip of the abdomen are especially vigorous and prolonged. A number of wasps of diverse groups, following final closure of the nest, pick up sticks, seeds, and pebbles and place them over the filled burrow.

It has been noted that in certain wasps much of the soil for closure (temporary or permanent) is dug from one or a few spots near the entrance, resulting in a small hole or quarry. This is especially true in species which nest in relatively hard soil. There is evidence that in some cases these quarries (which remain open and visible after the nest entrance is closed) divert the attention of parasites; that is, bombyliid flies may lay their eggs in them or mutillids may spend time digging at the bottom of them. In several wasps of diverse groups, similar holes are dug either before or after closure and evidently are not quarries at all but purely devices for deterring parasites. This behavior has thus been divorced from its original function and its original position in the cycle of behavior. Such "accessory burrows" are a fixed feature of the behavior of certain species of *Sphex, Bembix, Philanthus,* and other genera. Usually one or two are constructed close beside the true nest entrance, and to a depth of anywhere from a fraction of a centimeter to 10-15 centimeters; but some species occasionally make as many as five such burrows (Figs. 58, 59). In every case these accessory burrows are left open and the true burrow closed. Wasps often renew these burrows when they become accidentally filled, and in a few cases females or even males have been observed to rest in them, but in general they are "ignored" by the wasps.

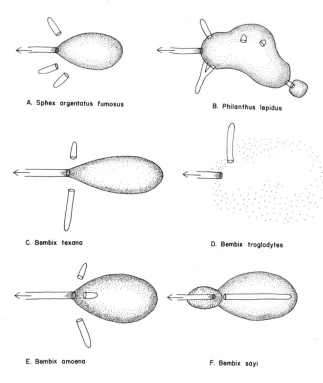

A. Sphex argentatus fumosus

B. Philanthus lepidus

C. Bembix texana

D. Bembix troglodytes

E. Bembix amoena

F. Bembix sayi

FIG. 58. Accessory burrows of six species of Sphecidae, in each case with the true burrow toward the left (direction indicated by an arrow). In *Bembix troglodytes* the accessory burrow is dug after the mound of earth at the entrance has been leveled, while in *Bembix sayi* it is dug beneath the mound.

Nesters in Hollow Twigs and Other Cavities

Quite a number of solitary wasps are not diggers but make use of natural cavities, especially tubular cavities such as abandoned beetle borings or hollow, dead sumac twigs, and so forth. These wasps are often called "renters," since they expropriate a ready-made niche, and in such niches several species may succeed one another. Many solitary bees also nest in tubular cavities, and the competition among the various twig-nesting bees and wasps must at times be severe, as it is among birds that nest in cavities in wood.

FIG. 59. Top figure, a female *Bembix texana* carries prey to a closed nest entrance between two open accessory burrows. Bottom figure, a parasitic mutillid wasp walks across a closed *Bembix texana* nest after leaving one accessory burrow and before entering a second.

Two quite different groups of wasps make up the "rent-ers": a few primitive forms that probably never developed the ability to make a nest (some Bethylidae and a few

FIG. 60. Nest of a typical "renter," *Isodontia mexicana,* in a hollow sumac twig. This is a "grass-carrier," using grasses and plant fibers to make the plugs between the cells. The upper cells contain cocoons, the lower ones dried tree crickets (the wasp egg having failed to hatch in these cells).

Pompilidae and Sphecidae), and a vast assortment of gen-era (a few Pompilidae and many Sphecidae and Eumeni-dae) which are probably derived from nest builders. Members of the first group use diverse kinds of cavities in the soil, in plants, or even empty snail shells or the like; they often make only one cell, which is closed off with debris of some kind. Members of the second group typically make a series of cells, separated by partitions, more or less filling the available space. There have been many publications on these wasps in the past few years, largely as a result of the development of the technique of "trap-nesting." A "trap nest" is simply a section of wood with a hole bored in one end, or a piece of sumac, elderberry, or other tree in which the pith has been removed. These are placed in a horizontal position in nature: in open woodland, thickets, hedgerows, around buildings, and so forth. They are accepted by a wide variety of wasps and bees that normally nest in hollow twigs, and the nest contents can be readily studied by splitting the trap lengthwise with a knife. Further details of the technique, and many examples of the results which can be obtained, are included in Karl V. Krombein's book *Trap-nesting Wasps and Bees: Life-Histories, Nests, and Associates.*

A wasp that accepts a trap nest or a natural hollow twig first cleans out any wood fragments or other debris which may partially block the cavity. Then, in many cases, a plug is built against the inner end or at least near the end of the boring. The space next to it is then provisioned and the egg laid (or the egg laid first, in the case of Eumenidae). The completed cell is then closed by a partition and another cell begun against this partition. The number of cells is usually determined by the length of the available cavity, but in no case are cells constructed right up to the opening. Generally a vacant space, or vestibular cell, is left near the entrance, and this is closed off with a very thick closing plug (Fig. 61). Additional empty spaces, called intercalary cells, are sometimes interposed among the filled cells; since these are closed off with a thicker partition than usual, they are probably not simply empty brood cells but more comparable to the vestibular cell. Perhaps these empty cells, particularly the vestibular cell, play a role in deterring parasites, and are thus analogous to the accessory burrows of ground-nesters.

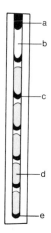

FIG. 61. Sketch of a typical "trap nest." *a,* closing plug; *b,* vestibular cell; *c,* cell partition, *d,* provisioned cell; *e,* preliminary plug. (After K.V. Krombein, 1967).

Various materials may be employed in making the partitions and the closing plug. These may be particles of dry substances which are packed into place or of moist material which dries to a hard plug. Dried materials include such things as earth, small pebbles, seeds, sawdust (often scraped from the boring), pith, pieces of leaves, grass blades, and so forth. Pompilidae of the genus *Dipogon* often build plugs consisting of alternate layers of such things as soil, bits of lichens or moss, droppings of caterpillars, and even the bodies of dead ants and other insects. Females of this genus have a pair of tufts of curved bristles beneath their head (hence the name *Dipogon,* or "two-beard"), and this device apparently aids in carrying diverse materials into the nest. These wasps have sometimes been seen collecting bits of spiderweb and taking them to the nest, and spider silk often makes up parts of the nest partitions.

Members of a tropical genus of Pompilidae, *Priochilus,* are reported to line their cells with pieces of leaves, the leaves being bent in such a way as to form the partitions. Members of the sphecid genus *Isodontia* are called "grass-carriers," since they are often seen flying with long blades

of grass trailing behind them. These wasps have a pair of
small flanges on their labrum which evidently assist in
holding the grass stems during flight. The partitions usually consist of short, compacted fibers, while the long closing plug is complex, consisting of compacted fibers, a section of coiled grass blades, and finally a section of straight
grass blades which protrude from the entrance. Karl
Krombein, in his extensive studies of North American
twig-nesters, found that in one species of *Isodontia, mexicana,* the partitions between the cells are flimsy or even
absent. In another species, *auripes,* there are apparently
no partitions at all, the wasp merely placing several eggs
and many paralyzed tree crickets in a single long chamber
(Fig. 63). Evidently the larvae are able to develop to maturity without serious cannibalism, although cannibalism
has been reported in some species of this genus. Such loss
of cell partitions is uncommon among wasps.

Other Sphecidae use particles of soil or wood or bits of
debris in their partitions. In some cases these materials
are sealed in with mud or plant resins. In the genus *Passaloecus,* the partitions and closing plug are built entirely
of plant resins, while in *Trypoxylon* they are built of mud,
that is, of soil particles held together with water or with

FIG. 62. A eumenid wasp carrying a small caterpillar into a trap
nest. In this instance four trap nests were taped together, two
facing each direction, and the block placed beneath the rafters
of a building.

salivary secretions of the wasps. In virtually all Eumenidae, the partitions are of mud.

The partitions and terminal plug serve several obvious functions: they prevent cannibalism among the wasp larvae, present obstacles to parasites and predators, and afford some protection from adverse weather conditions. They also serve at least one less obvious function. When the adult wasp emerges, it must break through successive partitions *toward* the open end of the boring; in at least some cases a wasp which heads in the wrong direction dies in fruitless attempts to dig through the wood at the blind end. K.W. Cooper has demonstrated by a series of simple experiments that the cell partitions convey the necessary information regarding direction. Since these partitions are built from the outer side, this side is rather smooth and slightly concave, while the inner side is rough and convex. When the larva spins its cocoon it orientates in such a way that it comes to rest facing the rough, convex wall and away from the smooth, concave wall. Thus the pupa and emerging adult are facing toward the open end of the boring. In a sense, the mother has "left a mes-

FIG. 63. A trap nest containing a large cell provisioned with crickets and containing four larvae of *Isodontia auripes*. This Floridian "grass carrier" has built its partitions of Spanish moss. (Photograph copyright Karl V. Krombein.)

sage" for her offspring which is vital to their survival. Since we know that ground-nesting wasps also orientate toward the rough and irregular closure of the cell and away from the smooth, concave inner end, it is evident that twig-nesters have inherited this trait from fossorial ancestors. The response of the larva to the cell closure is highly adaptive in either context (wasps emerging in the ground dig their way out more readily by way of the old burrow). Twig-nesters of diverse groups respond to similar cues in the cell partitions—and so do cuckoo wasps and other parasites.

When cells are in series in a boring, there would seem to be special problems of emergence, since the wasps toward the entrance must have evacuated their cells to permit emergence of the wasps in the inner cells. Yet the wasps in the inner cells develop from eggs laid somewhat earlier, and should therefore have matured first. Several factors work to insure that, in fact, wasps in the outer cells do usually leave the nest first. When adults first emerge from the pupal stage, they remain in the cells for 2–4 days while their integument and wings dry and harden. There is apparently a period of time during which they are capable of emerging but do so only in response to a stimulus, and it is believed that the vibration provided by a wasp chewing through the wall of an adjacent cell is such a stimulus. Furthermore, many twig-nesters produce females from the innermost cells, followed by a series of males in the cells toward the entrance. Since larval and pupal stages of the females are slightly longer than those of the males, the wasps in the inner cells are in fact not ready to emerge until the outermost cells have been evacuated.

Extensive studies with trap nests have shown that Eumenidae, in particular, generally make several female-producing cells followed by several that produce males. Cells which give rise to females are, on the average, larger in size and contain more food. For example, Krombein's studies of *Euodynerus foraminatus apopkensis* in Florida showed that in borings with a diameter of 6.4 mm, female-producing cells averaged 17.5 mm in length, male-producing cells 13.4 mm in length. In this species cells producing females averaged 14 paralyzed caterpillars per cell, while male-producing cells averaged only 8. In borings of this

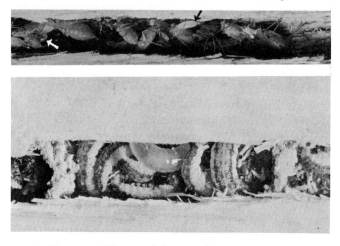

FIG. 64. Two very different inhabitants of trap nests in northeastern United States are *Passaloecus cuspidatus* (Sphecidae) (above) and *Ancistrocerus antilope* (Eumenidae) (below). *Passaloecus* provisions with aphids and makes very thin, translucent partitions of plant resins (a partition may be seen about halfway between the two eggs, which are marked with arrows). *Ancistrocerus* provisions with caterpillars and makes thick mud partitions; in this instance a wasp larva is seen in the cell. (Top photograph from Krombein, 1967).

diameter, somewhat more than half of 726 cells gave rise to females; but in borings 4.8 mm in diameter, over 90% of 825 cells gave rise to males: a reflection of the space limitation imposed by the narrow boring diameter. It is well known that male wasps are produced from unfertilized eggs, females from fertilized eggs, fertilization being controlled by the release or non-release of sperms from the spermatheca at the time of oviposition. In the case of

Eumenidae, the egg is laid before the cell is provisioned, but the female obviously "remembers" whether she has laid a fertilized or unfertilized egg. Evidently her depth within the burrow determines whether she will fertilize the egg, and this in turn influences the number of prey to be brought in and the final length of the cell.

This relationship between egg fertilization, size of the cell, and amount of food supplied apparently holds equally well for ground-nesting species, but it is much more difficult to study than in the case of twig-nesters which can be trap-nested in great numbers and whose nests are much more readily available for inspection. It should not be assumed that the sequence of sexes described above applies to all twig-nesters; some species of the sphecid genus *Trypoxylon,* for example, typically place male-producing cells at the inner end of the boring, female-producing cells toward the outer end. In the case of Pompilidae, which utilize a single spider per cell, a fertilized egg is usually deposited on larger spiders, an unfertilized, male-producing egg on smaller ones. In most wasps the adult males average considerably smaller than the females, but the reverse is true in the species exhibiting phoretic copulation discussed in the previous chapter.

As mentioned earlier, "renters" often take over cavities used earlier by another wasp and probably in some cases actually drive away a wasp or bee and fill the remainder of the cavity with their own cells. Hence trap nests are sometimes found to be occupied by more than one species of wasp or bee. Krombein mentions one nest in which a *Trypoxylon* had placed a paralyzed spider at the inner end of a boring, a eumenid (*Ancistrocerus catskill*) had then stored a cell, *Trypoxylon clavatum* stored cells 2–5, and finally *T. frigidum* cells 6 and 7. In another nest, a cell of *Euodynerus* was followed by a partially filled cell of a bee, and this in turn by several cells of another eumenid. The interaction of wasps and bees competing for borings has yet to be studied in detail.

The Building of Free Mud Nests

Members of several different groups of wasps have acquired the ability to construct nests wholly of mud, sometimes with the addition of other materials. The building of mud nests has been acquired independently by at least one stock of Pompilidae, at least two stocks of Sphecidae, and at least two (and perhaps more) stocks of Vespoidea. In some instances (for example, in the common black-and-yellow mud-dauber, *Sceliphron*) mud is collected from beside pools and puddles, while in others water is carried in the crop and used to moisten dry soil so as to form a moist pellet which is carried to the nest. Most Eumenidae take dry soil in this manner and can also be observed taking water, sometimes by alighting on the water and imbibing it through the surface film.

Mud-daubing in the Eumenidae may have evolved from situations in which water was carried to the nest and used to soften compacted soil, the wasp removing the earth in pellets which were at first discarded. The Hungarian entomologist Lászlo Móczár has made a detailed study of the eumenid *Paragymnomerus spiricornis,* which nests in the walls of vertical clay cliffs. The females take their water from damp rocks along a stream, carry it in their crop to the nesting site, and use it to moisten the clay before scooping it out with the mandibles; one load of water suffices for about 5 pellets. When adding a cell to the nest, the female carries out the majority of the pellets and simply drops them, in the manner of a typical ground-nesting "carrier." However, at other times these moist pellets are put to other uses. When a cell is fully provisioned, it is sealed off with a barrier of compacted mud, much like the partitions in the nests of twig-nesting eumenids. Even more interestingly, at the beginning stages of nesting, these wasps use the pellets to construct a chimneylike turret extending upward a distance of several centimeters from the entrance. At later stages, pellets may be used to

FIG. 65. A female *Paragymnomerus spiricornis* adding mud to the end of her turret rising from a vertical clay cliff. (László Móczár, 1960).

repair or strengthen the turret or to fortify the walls of the burrow. The function of this turret is poorly understood; there is little evidence that it deters parasites or that it protects the nest from heavy rains—in fact a severe storm may destroy most of the turrents. Some nesters in clay banks build turrets that are directed downward rather than up, and some species which nest in flat soil build turrets that extend above or along the surface of the soil. Certain ground-nesting bees build turrets remarkably sim-

ilar to those of Eumenidae, suggesting that these structures may have similar functions in the two groups.

It is but a short step from these wasps to such eumenids
as *Ancistrocerus waldenii,* which take over a crevice in
rocks—or sometimes the letters carved on gravestones—
where they prepare several mud cells, plastering them
over to form what appears to be merely a mass of earth.
Other eumenids have departed farther from the soil,
building clumps of mud cells on twigs. The true potter
wasps, of the genus *Eumenes,* build individual jug-shaped
cells, usually on twigs, often preparing several side by
side. Each "pot" has a funnellike entrance through which
the egg is laid and the prey introduced before it is finally
sealed over. Certain members of the family Pompilidae
have undergone a similar evolution in nest type. Some of
the common North American species of *Auplopus* build
individual mud cells under stones or fallen timber, while
certain tropical species attach clumps of mud cells to
twigs and branches.

Since eumenids and pompilids apply the moistened
earth in the form of a ball, their nests tend to have a
granular appearance from the outside. However, the inner
side is much smoother. When *Paragymnomerus spiricornis*
adds a pellet to its turret, it curves its body over the ball,
pressing against the inner side with the front of its head
while pulling the pellet from the outside with its legs
(Fig. 65). The ball of earth dries quickly, but subsequent
pellets are placed at different points on the edge of the
cell, presumably to assist in rapid desiccation. In *Eumenes,* and probably all potter wasps, the front of the
head is used to smooth the inner walls of the cell, leaving
the outer surface rough. Some Pompilidae, in contrast,
smooth the outer side (and probably also the inner side)
by curving their abdomen beneath and forward and using
the dorsal surface of the apical segment as a "trowel"
(Fig. 67); in the species of *Auplopus* this segment has a
smooth and polished area. Since Pompilidae which nest in

FIG. 66. A female *Paragymnomerus spiricornis* carrying a cater-pillar to her nest. (László Móczár, 1960).

the ground typically use the tip of the abdomen to press the soil in place at the time of closure, it is not surprising that the mud-users employ the abdomen in this manner, although such behavior is absent in the mud-using Eumenidae and Sphecidae.

In the Sphecidae, free mud nests are characteristic of *Sceliphron* and its allies, the so-called mud-daubers, and of a few species of *Trypoxylon*, which build parallel columns of cells and are often called "pipe-organ wasps" from the form of their nests. As mentioned earlier, the common black-and-yellow mud-daubers, *Sceliphron,* typically gather damp clay or loam from the margins of puddles or streams rather than "making their own" mud by water-carrying. The making of cells by these wasps has often been described and can be observed almost anywhere there is a porch, barn, or bridge presenting a suitable nesting site. Presumably *Sceliphron* originally nested in hollow trees or under cliffs, where in fact their nests are still sometimes found. Like *Polistes,* the paper wasp, *Sceliphron* has doubtless increased its abundance by taking advantage of man-made shelters.

Mud-daubers produce a loud buzzing sound both while gathering mud and while applying it to their nest, but so far as we know no one has explained the source or function of these sounds. Balls of mud are carried to the nesting site in the mandibles, and are applied with the mouthparts and the legs. The first few loads are smoothed out to provide a flat base. Subsequent loads are drawn out into

FIG. 67. A Philippine species of *Auplopus* (Pompilidae) smoothing over the surface of its nest by using its abdomen as a "trowel." (F.X. Williams, 1919).

erect arcs from this base, first to the right and then to the left, forming a cylindrical cell consisting of a series of half-arches which interlock on the outer side of the cell (Fig. 69). A cell is built during a period of intense activity over only an hour or two; some thirty to forty loads of mud are required to draw out one cell. A mud cap is added after

FIG. 68. *Eumenes pedunculatus* (Eumenidae) introducing a caterpillar into her jug-shaped nest among pine needles (above) and later bringing a ball of moistened earth with which to close the nest (below). (Both from Günter Olberg, 1959).

the cell is provisioned; if provisioning is not complete by evening, a thin, temporary cap may be provided until the following day. Additional cells are added beside and above the initial cell, generally forming a cluster of more or less parallel cells, often in two layers. More than 20 cells have occasionally been found in one nest, but the usual number is 4 to 10. Ultimately the entire nest is plastered with mud to form a somewhat irregular mass in which the individual cells are largely obscured. In the pipe-organ wasp, *Trypoxylon,* the cells are not smeared over in this manner, and the interlocking half-arches remain visible; in this instance parallel long tubes are constructed, each divided by partitions into several cells.

The nests of mud-daubers are often varicolored, reflecting different sources of mud during construction. An Asiatic species is said to cover the closing plugs with the faeces of birds and mammals. Old *Sceliphron* nests are often reused by various "renters," principally eumenids and pompilids, and these wasps often patch the nests with mud of other colors and textures. One of the principal renters of *Sceliphron* nests is the blue mud-dauber, *Chalybion.* The Missouri naturalist and storekeeper, Phil Rau, has pointed out that *Chalybion* is not a mud-carrier but a water-carrier, using the water to soften the adobe of old mud nests for patching or closing these for its own use. Members of both of these genera occur through most of the tropical and temperate parts of the globe, and it appears that in general species of *Sceliphron* are true mud-daubers, while the species of *Chalybion* reutilize various pre-existing cavities, closing them off with mud and sometimes with bits of excrement and debris. Phil Rau once observed a blue mud-dauber removing spiders from a *Sceliphron* nest, and he hypothesized that the blue mud-dauber was a parasite of the black-and-yellow species. However, his observations have never been confirmed except to the extent that both species will sometimes empty their cells of prey when seriously disturbed. The blue

FIG. 69. Above, a female *Sceliphron destillatorium* (Sphecidae) building one of the initial mud half-arches of which her nest will be built. (Photograph by László Móczár). Below, a nest of *Sceliphron caementarium*, showing the overlapping half-arches. The two cells at the center have been reused by an *Ancistrocerus* (Eumenidae), which has left an irregular clump of mud protruding from the cells. (Photograph by G.E. Bohart and W.P. Nye).

mud-dauber is more appropriately to be regarded as a "poor relative" of *Sceliphron* which either failed to evolve the architectural skills of that genus or has lost them; since it is able to "rent" a variety of niches as well as *Sceliphron* nests which may have been made during previous years, it is sometimes able to achieve a higher level of abundance than *Sceliphron*.

Some species of the potter-wasp genus *Eumenes* camouflage their nests with a paperlike outer covering made from wood fibers, bits of charcoal, pieces of lichen, and so forth. Some members of the eumenid genus *Zethus* build free nests on branches or vines consisting of clusters of cells built not of mud but of macerated leaves, plant fibers, and resins. It is from progenitors such as these that the paper nests of the social Vespidae may have evolved.

Since mud-daubers are easy to observe and to manipulate, they have often been used for experiments designed to demonstrate either the inflexibility of their instincts or various "intelligent" departures from stereotypy. The French naturalist Jean Henri Fabre once removed a *Sceliphron* nest just as the female was beginning to smear over the group of cells with a final layer of mud. The wasp continued to bring many loads of mud and to spread it, just as if she were "plastering her house", when in fact she was merely covering the spot where the nest had been. On the other hand, R.W.G. Hingston punctured holes in the mud pots of several eumenids and found that the wasps repaired them, even though this involved "a complete alteration in routine." Fabre concluded that his wasps were unable to adapt to new conditions because of the rigidity of their instincts, while Hingston concluded that "the potter understands the meaning of the problem, and deals with it in a rational way."

To the modern student of behavior, neither experiment is convincing and neither conclusion acceptable. Rather, he conceives of all behavior as having inherited components, not only relating to the performance of certain acts in certain ways but also permitting a certain flexibility of response to differing environmental situations. Thus insects are never complete automata; nor are they ever "ra-

FIG. 70. Above, nest of *Pseudomasaris edwardsii* (Masaridae) with three completed, capped cells and one incomplete cell. Below, individual cells of *Pseudomasaris edwardsii* are also seen to consist of overlapping half-arches, as in the very unrelated wasp *Sceliphron*, a remarkable example of evolutionary convergence. (Photographs by Philip F. Torchio).

tional." Rather, they are specialized to perform particular tasks with sufficient flexibility to permit survival in a somewhat changeable environment. The fact that insects sometimes do not respond to stimuli perfectly obvious to us while they perceive other things eluding us completely is often a product not of their greater "simplicity" but of their differently specialized sensory apparatus which, like ours, is adapted to receive a limited number of cues from the environment. Since the nesting behavior of the solitary wasps illustrates well the mixture of flexibility and stereotypy so characteristic of insects, it will pay us to take a sharper look at the nature of the behavior patterns we have reviewed.

Nesting Behavior as a Complex Instinct

The behavior patterns of solitary wasps are instinctive in the sense that they are performed in their complete, species-specific form in the absence of contact with parents or siblings. The adult wasp is able to mate, to seek nectar, and to clean itself as soon as it emerges, and after a short time (sometimes several days) the female begins to prepare a nest and to stock it with prey characteristic of her species. That does not mean that there may not be improvements in performance or that the wasp does not learn certain things—notably the nesting site and the location of food and of prey. But by and large it is acting out a life pattern like that of its parents and transmitted to it genetically. However, instinctive behavior is far from the simple running off of a set program, like a player piano; for behavior to "work" it must be paced to fill the physiological needs of the organism—food, sleep, a substrate for oviposition, and so forth—and it must harmonize with diverse and sometimes unpredictable environmental factors.

The preparation and provisioning of a nest is the most complex behavior performed by a wasp; in fact there are few better examples of complex behavior to be found in any invertebrate animal. It is assumed that the "brood-rearing instinct," like other instincts (mating, feeding, etc.), is under the influence of a "drive." That is, to speak somewhat loosely, the insect "feels a need" or is "in a mood" to prepare a nest and to deposit her egg within it. We do not know the origin of this drive. Some have assumed that the pressure of a maturing egg in the genital tract produces a condition akin to hunger or the need to void excrement, but unlike some insects (e.g., walking sticks) which simply drop their eggs, wasps are programmed to undertake a long series of actions not only up to the point of oviposition but well beyond it (to the closing of the cell). Evidence for and against the hypothesis that "egg pressure" provides a major source of "drive" is not clearcut. Many wasps prepare cells and provision rapidly under highly favorable conditions but are able to remain inactive for several days if the weather is unfavorable, suggesting that the act of oviposition is subordinate to other conditions and not a fixed periodic requirement. We know that the gonadotrophic hormone, secreted by the corpora allata, just behind the brain, influences egg maturation and related behavior in various insects, but the activation of the corpora allata may itself be dependent upon diverse factors such as mating, food intake, and light or chemical stimulation. It is entirely possible that "drive" is a reflection of hormone concentration, and that the latter is determined by a complex of previously received internal and external stimuli, but these are matters poorly understood at the present time.

It is usually conceived that the nesting and brood-rearing drive sets in motion a specific pattern of activities, each element of which is under the control of a subordinate drive. The pattern is characteristic of species, genera, or higher groups: for example, most Pompilidae hunt spiders before making a nest, while *Sceliphron* hunts spiders only after completing an elaborate nest-building procedure. Also, the movements and responses of each of these activities are species-specific, although allowing a measure of plasticity. *Sceliphron caementarium* (the black and yellow mud dauber) hunts primarily on plants and takes a great many crab-spiders, orb-weavers, and jumping spiders. *Chalybion californicum* (the blue mud dauber), on the other hand, hunts primarily on the ground or in stone piles, and tends to take a majority of theridiids, or comb-footed spiders, often including many black widows. That each species of wasp makes a nest of characteristic form is obvious enough from what has already been said; yet each is capable of a degree of latitude as to the precise form of the nest. However, a wasp in a "nest-building mood" is largely incapable of either departing grossly from its species-specific digging or masonry behavior or suddenly switching to some other phase of its behavioral cycle. For example, if prey is presented to a *Bembix* which is digging or closing a nest, it is generally ignored; if prey is carefully taken away from an *Ammophila* traveling toward her nest, she may continue until she reaches the nest entrance. Most cases of "blindness of instinct" which have been described are the result of wasps failing to adapt to a given situation when under the influence of an inappropriate drive. It is interesting to note that the described instances of nest repair by potter wasps involve a delayed response; evidently the interruption of provisioning must lead to a lowering of threshold for reactivation of building behavior. Also, all wasps probably have some innate capacity to repair damaged nests; without such capacity they would be seriously handicapped. How a wasp will respond to a given situation depends upon many subtle factors: the intensity of the drive, the quality and timing of the stimuli provided, the wasp's innate plasticity with respect to that facet of behavior, its capacity for learning and the frequency with which the new situation is encountered, and so forth. It is probable that many wasps have "latent" motor patterns which are activated only under certain conditions. The time is long since past when it is worthwhile to speculate whether behavior is "intelligent" or "instinctive"; what is needed are experiments to determine the causation of behavior in specific situations.

A major step in this direction was made in 1941 by the Dutch entomologist G.P. Baerends, who was working on *Ammophila pubescens* (called by him *campestris*). Like other species of its genus, this wasp makes shallow nests in the soil and provisions them with caterpillars, in this case progressively (i.e., over several days, as the larva grows). Baerends found it possible to replace the nest with an artificial one made of plaster of Paris, which could be opened at will (Fig. 71). He was thus able to change the cell contents and in this way learn their stimulus value. He found that on the first visit to the nest each day, the female "inspects" the cell, and this "sets" her behavior with respect to the nest for the remainder of the day. That is, if she finds a very small larva, she brings in from one to three caterpillars that day; if she finds a larger larva, she brings in three to seven caterpillars; if she finds a fully grown larva that is spinning its cocoon, she closes the nest and begins another one. However, after this inspection visit her behavior is not at all influenced by the cell contents. For example, if all the caterpillars are removed *after*

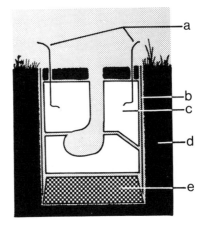

FIG. 71. Cross-section of an artificial *Ammophila* nest employed by G.P. Baerends for studying the influence of cell contents on behavior. *a,* wire hooks for lifting off top of nest; *b,* metal cylinder; *c,* plaster of Paris nest (in an upper and a lower section); *d,* soil surrounding nest; *e,* cork bottom. (After G.P. Baerends, 1941).

the inspection visit, she continues to bring in only the number required on the basis of her inspection, and may even make a permanent closure of a nest that had all its cell contents removed following the inspection. Thus provisioning behavior is paced to meet the needs of the growing larva by stimuli received only at one point in the behavioral cycle.

It is likely that each step in the unfolding behavior patterns is guided by such "sign stimuli." Although experimental evidence is still scanty, it is possible to present the nesting and brood-rearing instinct as a model in which each motor pattern is performed in genetically determined sequence, but only in the presence of the appropriate releaser (Fig. 72). In some cases, alternate pathways are possible, depending upon the nature of the releasing stimuli, and probably every action is capable of some adjustment to meet the releasing situation, some more so than others. For example, when *Bembix* brings in a very large fly, it may become stuck in the nest entrance, and when this happens the wasp may release its usual grip, turn around, and pull the prey into and down the burrow with its mandibles. Although oviposition is one of the most fixed aspects of behavior, A. L. Steiner showed that if that portion of the cricket on which *Liris nigra* normally lays its egg is carefully excised, after a delay the wasp will oviposit on another part of the cricket.

The model presented in Fig. 72 is for a mass-provisioner, which stocks the cell all at once rather than over several days as in *Ammophila pubescens,* and which maintains a single one-celled nest at a time. This model might fit in a general way some of our common digger wasps of fairly simple behavior such as the stink-bug hunter *Bicyrtes quadrifasciata.* With modifications, the scheme might be applied to any solitary wasp, and use of models of this kind may assist in designing relevant experiments or in focusing observations on critical points.

FIG. 72. Model of the nesting instinct of a solitary wasp (Evans, 1966, adapted from various sources). Presumed releasers are shown in small letters, fixed actions in capitals.

In practice, students of comparative behavior have found it convenient to treat major aspects of the nesting cycle as units ("nest construction," "hunting," and so forth). One may then compare aspects of each unit from species to species or compare the sequence of units in various major groups. The comparative approach to wasp behavior owes much to the pioneering efforts of the Japanese entomologist Kunio Iwata, whose monumental treatise in 1942 has done much to direct research since that time.

Comparison of the gross features of the nesting behavior of various wasps teaches us much about the evolution of wasps and the origin of various aspects of their complex behavior as well as that of their relatives the ants and the bees. Since in the next two chapters we wish to consider sociality among wasps, it is useful to think of the wasps as having undergone a series of behavioral changes which preadapted them for social life. However, this is not to say that all wasps are moving toward sociality or that the social wasps are in some sense more "successful"; for solitary wasps make up a far greater number of species, and even some kinds exhibiting very simple nesting behavior—for example, some of the Tiphiidae—are sometimes exceedingly abundant. The diverse types that have evolved reflect the fact that in the course of time wasps have found new ways to exploit their environment and have thus been able to thrive in a changing and highly competitive world. Among the major adaptations achieved by wasps in relatively recent geologic time may be mentioned the exploitation of modern and expanding groups of insects as prey (flies, for example); the making of deep, complex nests in the soil, permitting survival under rigorous environmental conditions (e.g., in deserts) or in spite of heavy parasite pressure; the development of free aerial nests of various kinds; and of course sociality.

Preadaptations for Sociality

Social life appears in many groups having separate ancestries, indicating that it has arisen many times in the Hymenoptera but only once elsewhere in the insects (the termites). Evidently the higher Hymenoptera are somehow preadapted for social life, and since ants and bees are believed to have been derived from wasplike ancestors, it is possible that the wasps hold the key to an understanding of this problem. It is probable that the haploid-diploid mode of sex determination, which is so characteristic of Hymenoptera, provided one major preadaptation, which we shall explore further in Chapter V. Another prerequisite is the possession of a nest, and furthermore of a nest which is dug before provisioning begins and which has several cells which are stocked with numerous prey. It is this facet of the problem that we wish to consider here.

The fact that several groups of wasps (Scolioidea, Pompilidae) do not build nest-cells to which they return repeatedly helps explain why none of them have become social; yet in a measure they may suggest evolutionary stages through which the social wasps may once have passed. A brief summary of the apparent major steps in the evolution of nesting behavior of solitary wasps may assist in an understanding of the origin of sociality. These steps are progressive in the sense that they must occur in approximately this order and that they lead from simple to more complex behavior. They may be thought of as "rungs in the social ladder" in the sense that the social wasps must once have "climbed" them (Fig. 75); but of course each rung must have its own adaptive value, since many wasps inhabit each rung successfully and the evolution of sociality was by no means preordained.

(1) Prey-egg. Wasps are believed to be derived from parasitoid ancestors, and some behave much like parasitoids, simply finding prey, stinging it, and laying their egg upon it, the prey usually recovering and resuming its normal activities until it succumbs to the feeding of the growing wasp grub. There is no nest at all. In some cases the prey is free-living (e.g., the leafhoppers attacked by Dryinidae, or spiders attacked by Pompilidae of the genera *Notocyphus* and *Minagenia*) and in other cases it is in a concealed situation (e.g., the beetle grubs attacked by many Tiphiidae and Bethylidae).

(2) Prey-niche-egg-(closure). In some cases prey which is sought out in its own burrow may be encountered outside its burrow and then dragged back in (e.g., Tiphiidae of the genus *Methocha*, Fig. 38); other wasps characteristically use the host's burrow for their nest (Pompilidae of the genus *Aporus*) or drag the prey into any available niche (many Bethylidae). Such wasps usually make some type of closure of the niche or the host's burrow. Wasps of this group often paralyze the prey permanently, and concealment of the prey doubtless protects it from diverse predators and parasites.

(3) Prey-nest-egg-closure. The term "nest" implies some prior preparation as well as a more or less thorough closure following oviposition. The simplest nest is a pre-existing hole which is cleaned out or expanded; a somewhat more advanced type is a simple cell dug from the wall of a burrow made by a mammal or another wasp; or the nest may be a burrow dug in the soil and terminating in a cell. Good examples of all three conditions occur in the spider wasps (Pompilidae), and a few genera of digger wasps

(*Prionyx, Podalonia*) also make shallow, unicellular nests following prey capture. Construction of these simple nests usually takes a short time (often an hour or two) and provides great protection to the prey and the developing wasp larva. The nest is usually dug not far from the point of prey capture and the prey left on the ground or hidden during nest construction.

(4a). Nest-prey-egg-closure. This involves a major rearrangement in the behavioral sequence, for the nest is made *before* hunting is initiated. In many cases the nest is dug in an area of bare soil which may serve as the site of a nesting aggregation year after year; but the wasps may hunt in a wide area in the surroundings. These wasps must be able to locate the nest readily when returning with prey. Obvious advantages are that the nesting and hunting sites need not be close together and there is no need to leave the prey while the nest is dug, thus exposing it to predators. Good examples are to be found among the spider wasps (e.g. *Pompilus plumbeus*) and the digger wasps (e.g. *Ammophila procera*). This rearrangement of behavior preadapted wasps for the making of multicellular nests, for once they became localized in a nesting area discrete from the hunting grounds it often became expeditious to make several cells from one burrow rather than successive separate nests (especially in areas of hard soil). This variation may be described as follows:

(4b). Nest-prey-egg-[cell closed & new cell prepared-prey-egg][n]-closure.[1] This subtype occurs principally if not exclusively in certain Pompilidae, some of which make multicellular nests in the ground, others in hollow twigs, and a few of which make clusters of mud cells. In the Philippine wasp *Paragenia argentifrons,* several females nest together without notable aggression and even re-use

---

1. Superscript (n) follows a portion of the behavioral sequence (enclosed in parentheses or brackets) which may be repeated a number (n) of times.

old cells. Evidently females live long enough so that their lives overlap those of their offspring, but there is no evidence that the females in these aggregations act other than as solitary wasps. No Pompilidae are known to have departed from the use of one prey per cell (thus making progressive provisioning impossible) and only a very few are known to nest gregariously or to live long enough to come in contact with their offspring. We may therefore leave the Pompilidae on this "rung of the social ladder."

(5a). Nest-prey-egg-(prey)^n-closure. A great many digger wasps (Sphecidae) lay their egg on a small prey and then continue to fill the cell with small prey before closure; thus they are relieved of the necessity of carrying prey of their own (large) size but can range widely and carry their prey swiftly on the wing. Examples are to be found in such genera as *Ammophila* and *Bicyrtes;* this is essentially the pattern we have outlined in Figure 72. Two common variations on this pattern are as follows:

(5b). Nest-prey-egg-(prey)^n-[cell closed and new cell prepared-prey-egg-(prey)^n]^n-closure. That is, the wasp makes not one but a series of cells. Species of some genera (e.g. *Bicyrtes*) make either unicellular or multicellular nests, perhaps dependent upon the rate at which they are able to capture prey. Members of such genera as *Sphex* and *Stictiella* apparently always make multicellular nests and oviposit on the first prey in the cell. Much more commonly, however, the egg is laid on one of the *last* prey placed in the cell, in the following pattern:

(5c). Nest-(prey)^n-egg-[cell closed and new cell prepared-(prey)^n-egg]^n-closure. This is the manner of nesting of such common genera as *Gorytes, Philanthus, Cerceris, Crabro,* and many others. It is noteworthy that it is essentially a "dead end" so far as the development of progressive provisioning is concerned, for a wasp cannot provision a nest progressively unless the egg has been laid on the first prey or in the empty cell. The presumed selective advantage of this nesting pattern is that the wasp can, in a period of prey scarcity, fill a cell over a period of several days before laying her egg, or conversely, can fill several cells rapidly when prey is abundant and yet space her egg laying over several days.

(6a). Nest-prey-egg-(prey)^x-closure. In this instance, "x" is used to denote the fact that additional prey are brought in over several days, the number per day being graded in accordance with the size of the larva, probably via "inspection trips" as described by Baerends in *Ammophila pubescens*. The species of *Ammophila* and most species of *Bembix* make a series of closely grouped unicellular nests; but other wasps (including some species of *Bembix*) make multicellular nests:

(6b). Nest-prey-egg-(prey)^x-[cell closed and new cell dug-prey-egg-(prey)^x]^n-closure. Progressive provisioning involves considerable contact between adult and larva, and it is assumed that its selective advantage lies in the greater protection from parasites, predators, and nest scavengers afforded the larva. Some progressive provisioners actually clean the cells of debris at frequent intervals, and such evidence as we have suggests that in fact the incidence of parasitism, at least by miltogrammine flies, is very low in these insects. Of course, the number of eggs laid is greatly reduced, since the female spends several days at one cell, and in fact the ovaries of progressive provisioners characteristically produce eggs at a slower pace than in mass provisioners. It is interesting that in at least two species of the large genus *Ammophila* the female maintains more than one nest at a time, thus allowing a more rapid rate of oviposition, and in two species of the large genus *Bembix* females are reported to begin a new cell before the previous one is fully provisioned. In such instances, it is conceivable that a female might live long enough to come in contact with her own adult offspring, although in fact there is no evidence of this occurring in this genus.

It is often assumed that progressive provisioning arose from "delayed provisioning," that is from a situation in which provisioning was not complete "on schedule" as a result of inclement weather or prey scarcity, and that it became established in certain stocks of wasps because of the advantages afforded in protecting the larva. Delayed provisioning has been described in *Bicyrtes*, a genus related to *Bembix*, as well as in some species of *Ammophila*.

(7a). Nest-egg-(prey)^x-closure. A very few Sphecidae, chiefly a few species of *Bembix* and related genera, lay their egg not on the first prey but in the empty cell. The assumed advantage of this is that the female is freed from the necessity of hunting for prey before ovipositing and from the danger of introducing the maggots of miltogrammine flies when the egg is present (at this stage they invariably kill the host, but this is not necessarily so when the wasp larva is larger). So far as known, none of the digger wasps exhibiting this behavior make multicellular nests, although there seems to be no reason for their not doing so.

None of the Sphecidae has gone beyond step 7 in "the social ladder," even though this is by far the largest family of wasps. Why they have gone no further must remain an enigma; one major factor may be that the lifespan of the female is rarely sufficient to overlap that of her offspring. There are, however, a few cases of near-sociality and one of perhaps true sociality in the Sphecidae, and these will be worth a closer look before we proceed.

Students of bees believe that sociality in that group has arisen via two routes: by way of mother-daughter associations and by way of compact nesting aggregations in which females of the same generation share a common burrow and eventually develop a division of labor. Several groups of Sphecidae and even Pompilidae such as *Paragenia* show the beginning stages of mother-daughter associations, a route followed by the Vespidae to a much greater extent. The Italian entomologist Guido Grandi has found that in fact the nests of the digger wasp *Cerceris rubida* may contain, toward the end of the season, an old mother and four or five adult daughters, all living together amicably and evidently "taking turns" at guarding the nest entrance.

The second route—that of gregarious nesters sharing common burrows, though all of the same generation—has also been followed by certain Sphecidae. *Moniaecera asperata* and several other members of the tribe to which it belongs (Crabronini) have been shown to be communal nesters, several females sharing a common burrow, presumably, however, building their own individual cells. Quite recently Robert Matthews has shown that *Microstigmus comes,* an inhabitant of tropical forests that builds nests pendant from beneath leaves, maintains communal nests with occasionally as many as 18 adults of both sexes in one nest. There is evidence that females cooperate in provisioning a cell, in guarding the nest, and probably in

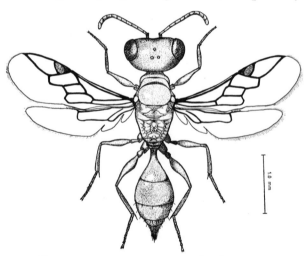

FIG. 73. *Microstigmus comes,* a minute sphecid wasp occurring in tropical rain forests that may represent the closest approach to sociality by members of its family. (R.W. Matthews, 1968).

FIG. 74. A nest of *Microstigmus comes* suspended by a coiled pedicel from the underside of a *Crysopila* frond. The nest is built of fibers scraped from the frond. (Photograph by C.W. Rettenmeyer; from Matthews, 1968).

building. Although the females show no obvious caste differentiation, dissection revealed that in each nest one female had one or two oocytes (immature eggs) larger than those of any of her nest-mates, suggesting that in each nest one female (an incipient "queen") may do most or all of the egg laying. Thus this species, and undoubtedly others of its genus, can be regarded as truly social. Matthews believes that the occupants of one nest may be members of one generation plus their newly emerged offspring.

It is of interest that both *Microstigmus* and *Cerceris* are mass-provisioners (like halictine bees), although the Vespidae evidently evolved sociality via mother-daughter associations involving progressive provisioning and direct feeding of the larvae. Obviously it is an oversimplification to portray "the social ladder" as a simple step-wise progression with no alternative routes, as Fig. 75 may imply. We shall examine these alternate routes in greater detail in Chapter V. In the meantime, we must place the Vespoidea with respect to the behavioral features we have been considering in this chapter. It is assumed that the ancestors of the Vespoidea must have passed through various intermediate stages not unlike those we have just outlined, although in fact the most generalized group, the Eumenidae, already shares many features in common with the "highest" Sphecidae: most notably multicellular nests with oviposition in the empty cell. However, most eumenids are mass-provisioners, and thus not strictly comparable to *Bembix* and its allies. We may regard them as belonging on step 7 of our series, but with some differences from the sphecids on that step:

(7b). Nest-egg-$(prey)^n$-[cell closed & new cell prepared-egg-$(prey)^n]^n$-closure. As mentioned earlier, eumenids typically use mud in some phase of their nesting, and this may have preadapted them for the construction of free aerial nests. Many eumenids suspend the egg from a delicate filament from the roof of the empty cell, possibly a mechanism for keeping the egg from a moist substrate or insuring that the newly-hatched larva is surrounded with fresh prey. A few Eumenidae are reported to exhibit "delayed provisioning" similar to that found in sphecid genera such as *Bicyrtes*. For example, the African mason wasp *Synagris spiniventris* is said to provision slowly during periods of prey scarcity, often bringing in the last prey when the larva is fairly large, although the cell is filled promptly at other times. A related species, *Synagris calida*, like a few other Eumenidae, has developed true progressive provisioning. Another important step was taken when still another wasp of this same genus, *Synagris cornuta*, developed the practice of chewing up the prey and presenting it to the larva in a macerated condition. This may be regarded as an important new step in our progression, although involving no major changes in the sequence of behavior, and we shall designate it simply as:

(8). Prey maceration. The beginnings of this behavior may be seen in many eumenids and even in some sphecids, which partially macerate (soften by chewing) the prey either for feeding purposes (malaxation) or perhaps to assist in immobilizing the prey. This may have permitted the evolution of potent, pain-producing venoms (and of the defensive behavior so characteristic of the Vespidae) by making it unnecessary to restrict the potency of the venom so that it would paralyze but not kill prey. Besides *Synagris cornuta*, a few species of the vespid subfamily Stenogastrinae may be said to be at this stage, nesting solitarily but feeding their larvae on a "gelatinous paste."

(9). Prey maceration combined with communal nesting, each female laying eggs and caring for her own larvae. Certain little-studied species of the Oriental genus *Stenogaster* may exhibit this behavior, but how much division of labor occurs or whether females occupying a nest are mothers and daughters or co-operating foundresses of the

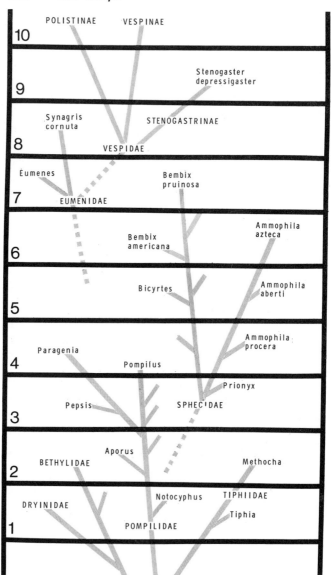

FIG. 75. "The social ladder." Only a few genera or higher taxa representative of each step are shown. See text for meaning of numbers of each step.

same generation is unknown. It is obviously a short step from such wasps to true sociality:

(10). Females supply food in accordance with stimuli received from the larvae and may feed larvae other than their own. Once this had occurred, natural selection tended to produce a familial society in which the most capable egg-layers became established as "queens" and others as "workers." Some of our most familiar wasps are social—as well as a great many less familiar tropical species—and we shall discuss them at some length in the next two chapters. The most familiar of all, the paper wasps of the genus *Polistes*, exhibit a fairly simple type of sociality, and it is appropriate that we look at them first.

IV. *The Social Paper Wasps:* Polistes

As far as most people are concerned, the "paper wasps" (Vespidae) are *the* wasps. This family includes most of the species that terrorize housewives, ruin picnics, and build the large aerial nests that challenge fleet-footed stone-throwing boys the world over. In short, the vespids are the wasps that commonly sting people, although ironically, their "unsociable" behavior is directly connected with the fact that they are "social" wasps—living in colonies with cooperative brood rearing. The sting used by solitary species in prey capture has in the colony dwellers become a weapon for the defense of home and kin.

Vespids are called "paper wasps" because they characteristically build nests of pulp formed by mixing macerated plant fibers with fluid from the mouth. The similarity between the paper made by wasps and that made by humans is not an accident. Although paper was made from various vegetable fibers in the orient for centuries before men studied wasps, the western world learned the use of wood pulp in paper manufacture from observations of wasp behavior. The great French naturalist and physicist René Antoine Ferchault de Réaumur, one of the first scientific students of insect natural history, reported to the French Royal Academy in 1719 that wood pulp like that made by wasps might offer a remedy for the growing shortage of rag papers in an increasingly literate Europe. More than 40 years later a German preacher and part-time scientist named Jacob Christian Schäfer wrote an influential book on new methods of paper making, in which he cited Réaumur's suggestion and included a sample of paper made from wasps' nests and from various plants.

The paper wasps are divided into three subfamilies: the Stenogastrinae, subsocial wasps found in the Orient and Australia; the cosmopolitan Polistinae; and the Vespinae (yellow jackets and hornets). The most studied paper wasps belong to the genus *Polistes* of the Polistinae, for these wasps build easily observed nests having a single comb of hexagonal cells without an envelope—the small paper nests commonly found in barns and garages and beneath the eaves of houses. A great variety of activities and interactions take place in plain view on the tiny stage that is a *Polistes* nest; and the colony rarely contains more than two hundred adults, so that it is sometimes possible to follow the movements of all the inhabitants simultaneously. This visibility, and the fact that the range of temperate zone *Polistes* happens to overlap that of university biologists, helps to explain why the biology of *Polistes* is relatively well known. We shall use this genus to illustrate the way of life of the paper wasps, and then proceed in the following chapter to discuss their social relatives.

Colony Founding and Queen Determination

In the temperate climate of Europe and North America, *Polistes* colonies are founded in the spring by fertilized, overwintered females. These "foundresses" are the late-summer daughters of the previous year's queens. They have mated in autumn, then hibernated in groups or alone, secreting themselves in cracks and crevices of old logs, attics, and barns. Males never survive the winter, but their gametes do, in the form of a tightly packed bolus of dormant sperm stored in the spermatheca, or sperm sac, of the overwintering female. This intricate little structure —a pearly sphere only a quarter of a millimeter in diameter, equipped with various glands and valves whose precise functions have never been investigated—releases newly activated sperm each time an egg is laid. A *Polistes* queen thus has a constant supply of sperm without repeated matings.

A *Polistes* nest begins as a nondescript dab of pulp smeared by an egg-bearing female wasp beneath some horizontal surface. Near the center of this initial dab, pulp is eventually extended into a small stalactite, forming the stem, or pedicel, from which the nest will hang. When this stem is about a centimeter long the tip is broadened into a shallow cup—the first cell. Thus it is always possible to identify the oldest cell in a nest by finding the one attached to the original pedicel. Soon other cells are added. But first the female lays an egg in the new cell. This is the rule usually followed throughout the life of the colony: eggs are laid one per cell, and new cells are initiated only when there are no empty cells present. With the laying of the first egg the female is officially a queen—an egg-laying nest resident.

In some *Polistes* species the nest initiator is the only female present until the colony offspring begin to emerge. But in other species there are sometimes from two to ten such foundresses. Only one of the associated females will ultimately be a queen; the others, although fertilized, usually become workers which help raise the queen's young. Observations of marked wasps indicate that co-foundresses of a nest are often sisters. In tropical populations which nest year-around sisters simply move from a declining colony to a newly founded one nearby; in the temperate zone females evidently remember the site of their parental nest and return to it after hibernation. The significance of sibling cooperation for the evolution of social life will be discussed in Chapter V.

In multiple-foundress colonies the nest initiator does not always retain the queenship for the duration of the colony; nor do all of the foundresses lay eggs, as has been assumed by many observers. Instead there is a complicated process of queen determination involving some of

FIG. 76. Foundress queen (*Polistes annularis*) on a young nest. In her mandibles she carries the flesh of a caterpillar to be masticated and fed to the larvae.

the more spectacular behavior patterns of *Polistes* females. The key to understanding this process is realizing that the associated females vary in their ability to lay eggs; for one thing, some have larger ovaries than do others. Furthermore, associated with developed ovaries is a tendency to add cells to the nest—a type of building not to be confused with the enlargement of cells already present. So being a queen involves having developed ovaries, laying eggs, and initiating cells.

The nest initiator usually qualifies at least temporarily as a queen. But most of the other foundresses associated with her on a new nest do not: they generally are foragers which, however, sometimes add new cells to the nest. The situation is most interesting when one of these auxiliary foundresses begins laying eggs. There ensues a quiet contest of egg laying and egg eating, in which each contender eats the other's eggs and replaces them with her own. Eventually one outeats the other and becomes the

FIG. 77. Nests of *Polistes* species, showing differences in the number and placement of pedicels and in shape of the comb. *a, P. goeldii; b, P. canadensis infuscatus; c, P. annularis; d, P. major; e, P. flavus; f, P. fuscatus.*

sole ovipositor. No one knows for sure how a female is able to distinguish her own eggs from those of other females. One hypothesis is that she eats only newly laid eggs (recognizing them by, say, their wetness) and refrains from eating any egg if she has just laid one herself. This mode of queen determination may seem an extravagant waste of good eggs. But it has a peculiar advantage for the ultimate queen. By competing in this way rather than by overt means such as routing or attempting to kill challengers, the future queen traps a labor force; for the lingering egg-layers and would-be queens add cells to the nest as if it were their own, enabling the colony to grow much faster than it otherwise would. So it is not surprising that all of the temperate-zone *Polistes* species in which queen determination has been observed accomplish this by differential egg eating, enabling them to make the most of their short growing season; whereas in the one extensively studied tropical species (*P. canadensis*) queen determination involves overt fighting and threat behavior accompanied by cessation of nest growth lasting up to five weeks. Evidently the tropical wasps can afford the luxury of family conflicts in regions where no cold or wet season limits their activities.

Another phenomenon conspicuous during the period of queen determination is the formation of dominance hierarchies among the foundresses living together on a nest. Dominance hierarchies have long been recognized as important features of vertebrate behavior, but they were unknown in invertebrates until an Italian zoologist, Leo Pardi, discovered them among European *Polistes* wasps. Pardi found that when two wasps meet on the nest they usually interact for a few seconds rather than just passing each other by. It is usually possible to call one of the wasps "dominant" and the other "subordinate." Dominant individuals stand high off the nest, head and antennae raised, and often vigorously antennate or bite at the other. Subordinates, on the other hand, crouch down, keeping head and antennae low and immobile. If neither individual acts subordinate there is a great rearing up and clashing of antennae, sometimes leading to biting, boxerlike grappling with the front legs, and stinging. But even severe fights rarely, if ever, cause physical injury; and in the vast majority of cases one wasp very quickly acts submissive as if recognizing its station in life relative to others.

Pardi noticed that the foundress queen was always the alpha, or most dominant, female in the hierarchy formed on a new nest. And when he dissected females of known rank in hierarchies he found a correlation between ovary size and social rank. In a hierarchy of three, for example, the alpha, beta, and gamma females ranked one, two, and three in order of decreasing ovary size. Furthermore, the longer they lived together the more pronounced the internal difference became. Pardi hypothesized that this was due to another of the important facts he observed about dominance-subordinance behavior, namely, that dominant individuals are able to command solid food, regurgitated nectar, and pulp from subordinates. This would conserve

FIG. 78. Dominance and subordinance in *Polistes fuscatus*. The female on the left has the relatively elevated posture characteristic of a dominant individual as she aggressively bites a leg of a motionless, crouching subordinate (right).

the energy of a dominant female by making it unnecessary for her to leave the nest to obtain food and building materials, while costing the subordinates energy in replacing loads given up. Presumably these nutritional differences would affect the amounts of energy available for egg production, and hence would enhance differences in ovary size; and, assuming that the dominance differences are causally linked to the ovary differences, the larger ovaries would in turn be accompanied by greater dominance. All of this being the case, dominance relations would play a role in queen determination along with differential egg eating.

An established *Polistes* queen continues to forage occasionally, even when there is a large population of workers on the nest. But her trips are very infrequent (averaging less than one per day); and she almost invariably returns with pulp which she applies herself to a new, eggless cell. The subordinate foundresses are indistinguishable from the queen in physical appearance, but they function as workers—they do not lay eggs, they forage frequently, and they help care for the brood. Thus in *Polistes* the queen and worker castes are behavioral but not morphological categories. This is one of the reasons that *Polistes* wasps are considered "less highly social" than some other wasps (for example, yellow jackets and bald faced hornets, honeybees, most ants, and termites—species having castes with pronounced size differences or structural specialization).

Nest Building

While these interactions among the foundresses are going on, the nest—in temperate-zone species at least—continues to grow. Wasps get the plant fibers used in making pulp from a great variety of places, including dry weed and grass stems, fence posts, unpainted boards, dilapidated cardboard boxes, and old wicker chairs. The usual procedure in collecting the material is to walk slowly backward while rasping off a long strip with the mandibles. This is rolled into a ball beneath the thorax. The snapping of fibers makes a sound often audible several feet away, and being able to recognize the soft tick-tick of a wasp's jaws on wood is one of the exotic joys of being a wasp watcher.

The forager flies to the nest with the ball held in her mouth. Upon landing she begins rapidly moving about the face of the nest, antennating the nest surface and occasionally even moving her head along a cell perimeter as if adding pulp, but without doing so. Finally she settles down to extending the walls of a cell somewhat shallower than those adjacent to it—a practice that tends to keep the face of the nest planar. The fibers are simultaneously added to the nest and soaked with water regurgitated from the crop, at first forming a thick, lumpy rim of wet pulp at the edge of the cell. This crude addition is gradually mandible-tamped to uniform thickness, the builder working over and over the rim for several minutes. Then, as if having earned the luxury of a bath, she usually grooms briefly and moves on.

The mouth of the first cell is round. Its sides are gradually lengthened as the nest grows, and only when it is surrounded on all sides by other cells does it take on the

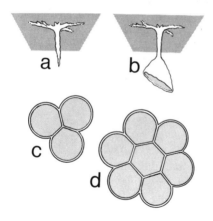

FIG. 79. The development of hexagonal cells. The nest begins as a pulp stalactite (a). The first cell (b) has a circular mouth, and develops straight sides when other cells are added (c). It becomes hexagonal in cross-section only when surrounded on all sides by other cells (d).

FIG. 80. Hexagonal symmetry in a nest of *Polistes flavus*. Cells contain larvae and glistening drops of nectar.

familiar hexagonal cell form of wasp and honeybee combs (Fig. 80). The hexagonal symmetry of these cells has intrigued mathematicians, philosophers, and biologists for centuries, so that today a bibliography of the subject includes such monumental names as Aristotle, Pliny, Kepler, Réaumur, Buffon, and Darwin.

The cells of bees and wasps were at the center of a major controversy between Charles Darwin and early critics of the evolution theory, the critics maintaining that only God could have been so ingenious as to endow insects with the power to construct such perfect and efficient shapes. In the present century numerous authors have speculated as to the means by which wasps and bees are able to build hexagons. D'Arcy Thompson, in *On Growth and Form,* compared the hexagons to those represented by contiguous soap bubbles and various plant and animal cells and suggested a physical explanation in terms of forces exerted by the expansion of adjacent spheres and cylinders. However elegant the armchair explanations, simple observation has shown that the workaday wasp, in ignorance of both God and physics, uses its antennae to guide the construction of hexagonal cells, whipping them about inside the cells adjacent to the wall being built, and forming straight lines equidistant between walls contacted. By always beginning cells in the groove between preexisting ones, and allowing adjacent cells to share sides rather than building each cell independently the wasp can with this guidance system achieve hexagons. Unshared cell sides remain circular in outline and a cylindrical cell reminiscent of those of mud daubers and certain potter wasps results, suggesting that the hexagonal form is derived from the cylindrical cells probably constructed by the solitary ancestors of *Polistes*.

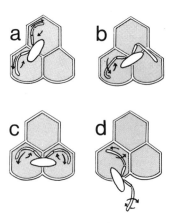

FIG. 81. Antennal movements during application of pulp to cell walls. The antennae stroke the sides of adjacent cells, one on each side of the wall being constructed (a). At a corner, one antenna moves into another cell (b) and application in a second plane results (c). On the periphery of the nest one antenna fails to contact a cell and an arc is constructed (d).

Bees, incidentally, probably use a different means of determining cell shape, since they evidently mold their cells by scraping and shaping the wax from inside the cell rather than straddling the wall as does a building wasp. Furthermore, they perform an architectural feat unknown in any wasp: the vertical combs are placed back-to-back so that the cells share bottoms as well as sides, making each cell bottom in the form of a trihedral pyramid. The bees' cells are thus perfect truncated rhombic dodecahedrons!

Development of the Eggs and Larvae

In contrast to the honeybee hive, in which certain cells contain brood and certain others are reserved for storage of honey and pollen, all of the cells in a *Polistes* nest are primarily brood cells. The egg is cemented in each new cell usually to the cell wall nearest the nest center, where it points toward the center of the cell. The transformation to larva occurs in about two weeks in the temperate zone and is barely discernible when the egg's free tip acquires motility and a mouth. The *Polistes* larva is little more than a sac for processing food. Not surprisingly, most of its behavioral responses have to do with food. It is unable to get out of its cell or even to turn around within it, but it can extend its head a few millimeters over the edge. This movement has become involved in a simple communication system between larvae and adults. When a female is dispensing solid food or nectar to larvae, she often finds them with bodies compressed and head retracted into the cell. She pauses at the mouth of the cell and signals her presence by rapidly knocking her head against the edge, the resulting vibration of the nest producing a brief buzz audible to the human ear. The larva responds by extending its body, bringing its mouth clear of the cell's edge. The adult then feeds the larva by thrusting material against it's face or, in the case of nectar, touching the larva's mouthparts with its own. The larva, in turn, reacts by exuding a drop of saliva and moving its mouthparts. In the transfer of solid food it is the larva that is then most active. It bites and tugs at the load held firmly by the adult until a morsel pulls free, then ingests it while the adult attends others.

The larval feeding reflexes are easy to elicit artificially. If the wall of a larva's cell is pricked sharply with a pin in imitation of head knocking, the larva protrudes its head. And if its mouthparts are then gently poked with the head of a pin a drop of clear fluid soon appears at the larva's mouth. The adults frequently move from cell to cell giving the feeding signals, then imbibing the drops of fluid thus elicited from the larvae—without giving any food in return. This interaction is the subject of one of those gentle controversies that make academic life interesting, while seldom causing any loss of life or limb. The first to observe the transfer of larval fluid was the French naturalist Etienne Roubaud, who described it in 1916 in a classic paper on African wasps. Roubaud, like some recent observers, had the impression that the adults avidly solicited the droplets, and considered the exchange of materials between adults and larvae a vital factor in the evolution of social life. This idea was given wide publicity later by the famed entomologist William Morton Wheeler, whose 1923 book *Social Life among the Insects* was for many years a standard in the field.

Even with this focusing on "trophallaxis," as such chemical communication came to be called, the role of the larval fluid in wasp social life is not understood. In 1952 M.V. and A.D. Brian studied the fluid secreted by larvae of *Vespula sylvestris,* a social vespid having *Polistes*-like larvae with a secretion solicited by the adults as in *Polistes.* They gathered samples of larval fluid and offered them to adults along with water and various kinds of sugar solutions and reported that the adults were not any more attracted to the larval fluid than they were to plain water. They suggested that the fluid may not be so much a social bond between adults and young as a means of excretion for a larva lacking a hindgut. However, chemical analysis has revealed that the fluid contains little in the way of nitrogenous wastes; and some as yet inconclusive studies suggest the presence of enzymes not produced by the adults but needed by them. So the controversy rages on, but one thing is certain: trophallaxis should not be considered in any sense a "prerequisite" for insect sociality, as the earlier workers implied. For some social insects—the stingless meliponine bees—manage their social lives without any larva-adult interaction, sealing the egg and a food supply in a waxen cell that remains closed until the young bee matures.

In temperate-zone *Polistes* the larval stage lasts, on an average, about 15 days. Its end is signaled by the appear-

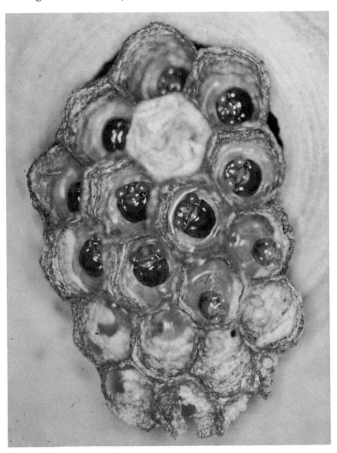

FIG. 82. Immature *Polistes* wasps (*P. canadensis*). Shallow peripheral cells (bottom) contain eggs; deeper central cells contain larvae. The white-capped cell contains a pupa whose silken cocoon (spun by the mature larva just before pupation) lines and closes its cell.

ance of a gleaming white silken cap over the cell, spun by the larva itself before pupation. The cell then becomes a cocoon where the wasp undergoes the transformation from grublike larva to winged adult. After about twenty-two days inside the capped cell, a fully pigmented adult emerges.

Behavior of Adult Females

For two to five days after emerging the young adult does little except groom (preening is a frequent activity of all adult *Polistes*), buzz its wings, and solicit an occasional mouthful of food from other adults. Then, or perhaps earlier—the mechanism is still a mystery—an important decision is made regarding a female's role in the colony (we shall deal with males later). As we have already seen, there are two behavioral castes in *Polistes:* the workers, which forage but generally do not lay eggs and the queens, which lay eggs and do little foraging. Corresponding to these castes there are two behavioral categories among the young females emerging on a nest. Some begin to forage after the brief callow period and are workers as long as they remain on the nest. Others remain lethargic and idle like the newly emerged ones, grooming and soliciting food, but spending most of the day and night crouched out of sight on top of the nest. They seldom leave the nest and never return with food, water, or pulp. Nor do they participate in the distribution of these materials to other individuals. Some of these non-workers are destined to be queens.

Technically, all a *Polistes* female has to do to be called a queen is lay eggs. Sometimes—when an established queen dies or dissappears from the nest—a worker begins to oviposit. And, as already pointed out, subordinate foundresses may lay eggs during the period of queen determination. However, reproduction of such temporary queens is probably negligible: workers seldom get a chance to lay eggs until the end of the season, when there is insufficient time for their offspring to mature. Even then they can produce only males, as they have not mated (even workers on nests with males for some reason do not mate). And most of the few eggs laid by subordinate foundresses are devoured by competitors. So the only queens of consequence are the alpha foundresses—the females who manage to dominate their companions on new nests and become the biological mothers of the next generation.

Becoming dominant in a group of foundresses is only the last in a whole series of trials leading to the queenship. Not the least of these for a temperate-zone wasp is making it through the winter; and to produce female offspring she must have mated the previous autumn. The non-workers have a number of advantages over workers in this competition for reproductive rights. Their relative inactivity means that they are able to store energy rather than consuming it in foraging and brood care. But probably even more important is the fact that the non-workers emerge late in the summer, whereas the workers are the first born of the colony offspring. Females emerging toward the end of the summer are more likely to persist until the autumn mating season, and are more likely to live through the winter. Furthermore, they tend to be better nourished and larger, as there is a gradual seasonal increase in the food available to larvae (due to a general rise in the worker: larva ratio and in the proportion of food in foraged loads). So the idle female offspring have been called *fondatrices-filles*—foundress daughters—in recognition of their enhanced likelihood of appearing on new nests the following spring. The behavior of these wasp ladies-in-waiting on the parental nest is a dull contrast to the bustling activity of their worker sisters.

In a typical day, an ordinary worker on a midsummer's nest in a midwestern barn makes about twenty foraging flights. When she is young she memorizes the location of her nest, circling and dipping about it, often hovering in a prolonged buzzing stare at a particular rafter or a conspicuous knothole. Inexperienced wasps who are prevented from doing this (for example, by being experimentally chased from the nest before their first flight) seldom make it back; and one of the hazards of artificially transplanting colonies is that some foragers fly off without executing these orientation flights, then never return, as they have the wrong set of homing cues. On the other hand, transplanted individuals who circle before leaving usually return home.

Polistes wasps forage for four different kinds of things: fiber for use in making pulp; proteinaceous food, usually

FIG. 83. Transfer of regurgitated fluid from one *Polistes* female to another (*P. fuscatus*). A viscous liquid, probably nectar, is visible between the mandibles of the solicitor (above).

in the form of insect larvae; nectar; and water. The females never collect and transport pollen. Hunting wasps are innocuous, preoccupied creatures, about as likely to attack a human being as they are to sting a bush or a tree trunk. When near the feeding places of caterpillars, *Polistes* females climb in a frenzy up and down branches or grass stems, often retracing their steps and seeming to leave no place unexplored. When they encounter prey they seize it immediately with their mandibles and, if the prey is small, fly off with it almost before a human observer notices the capture. *Polistes* wasps do not sting their prey unless threatened by it, as, for example, by the violent writhings of a large caterpillar. Instead they process it alive, chewing transportable chunks from large prey, and simply carrying off smaller captives. Upon arrival at the nest food masses are held by the front pair of legs and masticated for several minutes. During this process the mass of food appears to get smaller, either through compression or because the adult ingests a portion. Eventually one edge is pulled almost free of the load and thrust at the face of a larva. Usually, as explained above, the larva itself tugs this bite-sized piece away. But if the larva is unresponsive a worker sometimes pushes a load so forcefully that a bit of moist food adheres to the recalcitrant larva's face.

Returning foragers are frequently met upon landing by one or more of their adult nestmates, who chew simultaneously at the load until it separates into two or more chunks, which are then masticated and either ingested, shared with other adults, or fed to larvae. Foragers seldom resist such sharing, and a single foraged load may be divided among as many as seven adults. Pulp loads are never divided into several portions in this way, although they are sometimes solicited and transferred. Perhaps this is due to the advantage of adding a pulp load in an unbroken (hence stronger) piece; or perhaps it is simply because pulp is, after all, rather bland stuff to chew on.

It is difficult to estimate the amount of nectar fed to larvae, but it appears to be a major part of their diet. Wasps are common visitors of flowers, and sometimes take up juices from ripe or rotting fruit. In tropical South America they are famous pests at "trapiches," small factories where juice is pressed from sugar cane and boiled to make crude sugar cakes called "panela." Before the advent of insecticides the vertical combs of *Polistes canadensis* commonly hung like fringe along every rafter of the trapiches and the resident wasps "swarmed" at the edges of the wooden vats of syrup, earning for themselves the nickname "panelera." At the nest nectar is sometimes stored in egg-containing cells, in the form of viscous droplets regurgitated onto the cell wall. Sometimes several drops are placed in the same cell, and if not consumed they dry to form a hard sugar. But usually the drops disappear before the egg hatches or soon thereafter. One might expect to find the greatest stores of nectar at the end of the summer, in preparation for cold days. But sugar storage then takes a less communal form: on waning autumn nests the wasps are often found sitting with drops of sweet-tasting liquid glistening at their mouths. Occasionally the drops are sucked in, then slowly exuded again. The repeated regurgitation of the sugary solution may allow water to evaporate, making it possible for individuals to store an increasingly concentrated solution in the gut.

The gut also serves as a portable water tank. A dependable water supply is essential to *Polistes*, and when the wasps are present in arid regions it is a sure sign that there is a continuous source of water nearby—if not a stream or a cattle-watering tank, at least a patch of mud or a leaky faucet. Water is used in paper making, as mentioned above, and building wasps often collect water on their way to fiber-gathering sites. Workers of some species are able to alight and float on standing water while drinking; other species consistently drink at the water's edge.

On hot days many foraging trips are devoted exclusively to water collection. Droplets of water appear here and there on the nest and inside cells and some of the wasps sitting on the nest can be seen fanning their wings for minutes at a time. The combination of moistened nest surface and fanned breezes makes an effective evaporative cooling system, with a demonstrated ability to lower the nest temperature and, presumably, keep the brood from overheating. Even males and non-worker females, which ordinarily contribute little to the general welfare of the community, participate in the regulation of nest temperature by fanning.

Social insects have somehow gained the reputation of having highly organized, almost mechanically efficient communities. But years of scrutiny by highly trained and sometimes ingenious scientists have failed to reveal precisely how the insects manage to assure all chores being done at all times. In honeybees some light is shed on the matter by the finding that younger workers tend to labor in the hive whereas older ones forage. But no such relationship of age and duties performed can be shown in *Polistes*. Instead the paper wasps are noted individualists. One of the first biologists to observe the division of labor in *Polistes* was the gifted part-time naturalist Phil Rau, whom we have already mentioned in connection with his work on solitary wasps. Rau marked individual wasps with paint and recorded their activities, referring to them by what he called "Indian names" suggested by their marks. In Rau's observation colonies "blue dot" specialized in caterpillar hunting, and "white abdomen" was a water carrier. Certain marked workers are relatively aggressive, hence are more often involved in nest defense. But the roles of individuals change from day to day with no apparent regularity.

Like Darwin and Freud, the social insects have contributed to the disillusionment of man. For we now know that these "lower animals" communicate with each other, even exchanging information about such subtle things as the nature and location of food sources, thus claiming for themselves a capacity formerly considered uniquely human. *Polistes* wasps use a number of signals on the nest. One of them is the "head knocking" by workers on the sides of the cells of larvae, eliciting the body extension which is part of the larval feeding behavior. Another signal involving vibrations of the nest is the "parasite alarm."

Polistes nests are commonly attacked by females of the genus *Pachysomoides* (formerly called *Polistiphaga*), solitary parasitoid wasps of the family Ichneumonidae. *Pachysomoides* females can sometimes be seen sitting near nests awaiting their chance to oviposit. They then hop onto the nest, pierce the wall of a capped cell with the ovipositor, and inject their eggs. The parasite larvae—usually three to seven of them per parasitized cell—then consume the *Polistes* pupa and pupate there in its stead, shielded from discovery by the cocoon spun by their victim. The *Polistes* wasps seem to be incapable of recognizing a parasitized cell. Thus evidently the colony's only defense against this parasite is to prevent oviposition by the stealthy *Pachysomoides* females. Correspondingly, the survival of the parasite depends on its ability to escape notice prior to and during oviposition. So the approach of a parasite female to the nest is an event to which both species have been finely tuned by natural selection. The *Pachysomoides* female stalks a *Polistes* nest with great patience, moving forward only when the area near her is clear of alert *Polistes,* sometimes waiting immobile for several minutes for an opportunity to advance, then laying her eggs hastily and flitting away. The *Polistes* wasps, for their part, react vigorously to the discovery of a parasite near the nest. They dart toward it, chasing it from the nest at least temporarily, then continue darting about the nest in a fashion seen in no other situation. The jerky movements of an alarmed female cause the nest to vibrate audibly; this may serve as a signal, for other females begin displaying the same hyperaggressive behavior as the alarmist. The

FIG. 84. The behavior of a parasitic wasp (*Pachysomoides fulvus*) at a nest of *Polistes fuscatus*. The parasite female waits, immobile, near the nest (above). Then, when the area is relatively clear of adults, she hastily oviposits into a capped cell, where her young feed on the *Polistes* pupa (below).

alerted wasps move quickly over the face and top of the nest, carefully giving frequent attention to the nest periphery—where a parasite is most likely to reappear. This "parasite alarm" is also seen when certain parasitic flies appear near the nest.

The postures of encountering individuals are certainly communicative, a low crouch being a signal of subordinance and an elevated stance of dominance, the result usually being avoidance of overt fighting. The ability to signal relative dominance rank without prolonged or dangerous conflict is an important characteristic of the *Polistes* society, for it enforces with little loss of time or energy differences in function making for greater colony efficiency. Thus a queen (who can with her dominance signals command food and avoid foraging) is a more efficient egg-producer; and the foragers are probably more effective distributors of food since they are likely to pass it up the dominance scale toward the reproductive female. Although the possibility has not been thoroughly investigated, it appears that the degree of readiness of adults and larvae to solicit and accept food in itself is a kind of communication causing food to be directed to where it is most needed.

The Colony Cycle

A *Polistes* nest and the composition of the wasp population inhabiting it is always changing. In fact, a temperate-zone wasps' nest is a kind of calendar by which you can gauge the progress of the summer. Since old nests are rarely reused, inhabited nests in springtime are small and have shallow cells attended by one or a few females, the colony foundresses. In late spring and early summer there is a hub of bright-capped pupal cells in the center of the nest, which as they age become dark with lines of pulp spread across them by the adults. Soon the first offspring—almost invariably females—emerge from the capped central cells, and eggs take their places, leaving a ring of cocoons which gets further and further from the nest center as successively later young mature. The first twenty or thirty offspring to emerge are workers, that is, females who forage and care for the brood. Then the non-worker females and the males emerge, producing by late summer a large adult population composed mostly of future re-productives, which spend their days sitting, grooming, and soliciting food from returning foragers. In late summer, well before the onset of cold weather, the queen stops laying eggs and adds no new cells to the nest. But brood care proceeds as before and the adult population continues to grow as more offspring emerge.

FIG. 85. Cannibalization of the brood (*P. fuscatus*). A worker (right) first chewed away the cap of a pupal cell, extracted the young pupa as shown, and ate it, sharing the meat with other females and larvae.

With the cessation of egg laying the colony begins to show signs of decline. Cells from which brood has emerged or in which eggs or larvae have died are not oviposited in, and as a result there is an increasing number of empty cells. Late in the nesting season there is commonly some cannibalism of the brood by adults. Larvae and sometimes even pupae are pulled from the cells, then divided and fed to living larvae like foraged food loads. It has been suggested that this behavior may increase the number of young reaching adulthood by concentrating the dwindling resources of the colony in a few individuals. The scarcity of food is reflected in the behavior of wasps on the nest toward returning foragers: food-laden workers are solicited from with increasing vigor and are sometimes mobbed by seven or eight nestmates, all pulling at once at the bits of food held by the foragers' mouthparts. Even unladen returnees are met by solicitors.

Males are conspicuous on late summer nests. In many temperate-zone species the males have markedly curved antennae, and yellow faces and undersides which stand out in contrast to the dull female coloration (Fig. 88). *Polistes* males have the reputation of being idle liabilities on the nest. It is true that they do not bring foraged loads to the nest, and that they solicit and consume food which might otherwise go to the brood. And the males are social outcasts—the workers chase them about the nest, biting at them and often forcing them to leave, sometimes clamping onto a leg with their mandibles and dragging them some distance. But the males are not entirely useless to their society. They often fan their wings for long periods of time on hot days, thus presumably helping to lower the nest temperature; and they sometimes (though admittedly rarely) dispense solicited food to larvae. They are not entirely parasitic, since they frequently forage for themselves. In *P. canadensis* the males adopt an aggressive posture like that of alerted females upon approach of an intruder, thus probably contributing to the defense of nests.

As a result of the energetic chasing of males, the increasingly frantic mobbing of returning foragers, and the occasional pillaging of the brood, the colony takes on a disrupted appearance at the end of its growing season. Exiled males begin sitting in small groups off the nest. Later the entire adult population begins to disperse during the day, forming small clusters off the nest, then returning to spend the night at home. The brood wanes to a few shriveled larvae and some persistent pupae, their development retarded by the cold; and the nest is eventually abandoned by the adults. It is then that the males finally come into their own.

Mating and Hibernation

The males' primary *raison d'être* is sex. Even while on the nest they mount and attempt indiscriminately to copulate with individuals of both sexes. However most, if not all, successful mating activity takes place after the abandonment of the parental nest. Characteristically the males station themselves at a place frequented by females. Phil Rau observed a group of *P. rubiginosus* males attempting copulation with females emerging from a crevice which presumably led to a cavity containing a nest and was also a hibernation site. Males of *P. canadensis* in tropical Colombia have been observed in pursuit of females flying in and out of an abandoned coal mine containing numerous newly founded nests. And in *P. fuscatus,* the common brown paper wasp of North America, males sit near the entrances to hibernation places and pounce on the females as they enter. On sunny autumn days large numbers of this species sometimes gather, commonly flying about high sunlit structures near hibernation sites. These "swarms" of wasps look quite menacing. The males circle and dive as if attacking and pairs of wasps fall grappling to the ground. The mating wasps evidently remain coupled for only a few seconds at most. And they are in such active motion that it is impossible to observe the details of mating behavior or, in most cases, even to ascertain if copulation is complete. However, sexually responsive males, identifiable by their head-tilting alertness and their location near hibernacula, will copulate with females partially immobilized as shown in Figure 86, so it has been possible to photograph the movements involved in mating. Motion pictures indicate that the copulating male vibrates his antennae very rapidly against those of the female, and at one point uses the curled tips of his antennae to lift or stroke the female's antennae. Thus the antennae of *Polistes* males are morphologically and functionally reminis-

FIG. 86. Copulation of a male (above) and a partially immobilized female (*P. fuscatus*). During copulation the male's antennae beat rapidly against those of the female.

cent of those of certain male potter wasps. The latter are solitary relatives of the vespids in which the males of some species have sturdy hinged hooks at the extremities of their antennae (Fig. 87) which firmly grasp the antennae of the female during mating. The photographs also reveal

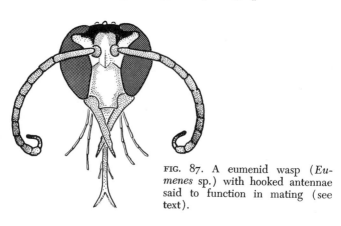

FIG. 87. A eumenid wasp (*Eumenes* sp.) with hooked antennae said to function in mating (see text).

that when the male genitalia are inserted the female's sting is extruded as it is, incidentally, when the genital orifice is open during egg-laying. Thus the attacklike courtship behavior of the *Polistes* male may be just that—an assault serving to elicit aggression and stinging by the female, thus moving the sting apparatus clear of the genital opening and making it possible for the male to insert his genitalia.

Some mating takes place in sheltered places near hibernation sites, where small groups of females sit prior to entering hibernacula, coming and going on warm fall days as they would to a nest. These pre-hibernation aggregations tighten and disperse with the variations in temperature of autumn days. Finally the females and an occasional long-lived male disappear into their hibernacula. Then, as an observant midwestern farmer told some university wasp hunters one frigid January day, "There ain't no wasps. It's winter."

The farmer was almost right about the wasps. Their deep torpor is a state very much like death. They are, as far as can be seen, absolutely unresponsive to light, and no amount of prodding evokes a detectable movement. They fall like corpses from their perches at the slightest touch; and they endure body temperatures well below zero degrees Fahrenheit—temperatures at which metabolism virtually ceases. The physiological adaptations enabling them to accomplish this are not well known. The wasps are dehydrated, which probably reduces tissue damage due to the expansion of freezing water; the small amount of blood present contains a natural antifreeze in the form of glycerine.

The function of hibernating in aggregations is not known. The groups break up in spring—they do not constitute a ready-made society for starting new nests. It might appear to warm-blooded humans that the wasps are huddling together to keep warm. But insects are thoroughgoing poikilotherms—cold-blooded creatures with no body heat to share. And, unlike overwintering honeybees, they do not buzz their wings to generate the heat that arises from muscular activity; in fact, it is probably advantageous for the wasps to keep cold, since they become active when warm and might thereby consume energy reserves essential for spring foraging and egglaying.

Biology of Tropical Species

Cold weather poses no problem for most *Polistes* wasps, for most of the more than 150 named species live in the tropics. Therefore the much-studied biology of temperate-zone species cannot be considered "typical" of *Polistes*. The tropical species are of particular interest to students of behavioral evolution. For the genus is thought to have originated in the tropics, and therefore the more primitive forms of polistine sociality are likely to be seen near the equator. Only one tropical species—ironically named *Polistes canadensis* because of a mixup about the collection locality of the earliest known specimen—has ever been studied in detail sufficient to permit comparison of its natural history with that of temperate zone species. The biology of equatorial populations of this species held some surprises for observers familiar only with north temperate species. For example, there was an apparent absence of males in hundreds of colonies observed in nature in all stages of development. But the whereabouts of the males was unknown until one day a mating pair was captured, revealing an almost complete absence of sexual dimorphism: the males were the same mahogany and black as the females, and lacked the distinctively curled antennae of the northern males (Fig. 88). With practice it was possible to distinguish the *P. canadensis* males from the females, and this led to a further interesting discovery. Males were common not only on mature nests, as expected, but also on newly founded nests—a situation impossible at high latitudes because the males succumb before spring nestfounding. Furthermore the tropical males were not attacked on the nest as in the north. It has been suggested that the *P. canadensis* males, lacking distinctive markings, are not recognized and chased from nests, where they may remain to mate with resident females (some dissected foundresses from newly-founded nests proved unfertilized and would therefore be potential

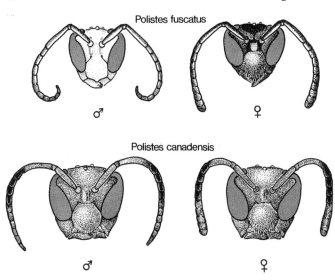

FIG. 88. Differing degrees of sexual dimorphism in two *Polistes* species.

mates). In the tropics it may be advantageous to tolerate males on nests housing unfertilized potential queens. On the other hand, in temperate-zone species it may be advantageous for males to be distinguished from females and chased from the nest so that they will mate only with females entering hibernacula (and hence likely to become queens the following spring). Viewed in this way, the sexual dimorphism of northern species appears to be a climatic adaptation. This hypothesis, like the explanation of differential egg eating, could not have been suggested from the study of northern species alone.

In the beautiful Cauca Valley of western Colombia, South America (4° N. latitude), *P. canadensis* starts new colonies at all times of the year, apparently unaffected by the slight seasonal fluctuations in temperature and rainfall. Life for these wasps, without the pressure of impending winter, moves at a relatively leisurely pace. Although the tropical nests seldom get much bigger than their temperate counterparts, the colony cycle is longer, evidently lasting six or seven months rather than the four or five months to which temperate species are limited. As pointed out above, there is sometimes a complete cessation of nest growth during the period of queen determination. And even when building activity is in full swing the colonies seem less active. The females, large dignified wasps with sluggish flight, commute to and from the nest for a few hours in the morning; then, like many forest creatures and some people, they take a midday siesta before a somewhat slower period of activity in the afternoon.

In spite of the generally higher and more constant temperature of its equatorial home, the average *P. canadensis* egg requires 68 days to produce an adult, whereas in two temperate zone species which have been studied the figure is only 48 days, making it possible to raise more offspring during the more compressed growing season in the north. *P. canadensis* also differs from temperate-zone wasps in having a sporadic production of worker females, rather than having all of the first-emerged female offspring become foragers. Probably the quick production of a work force by the overwintering species is a further means of accelerating colony growth during a short growing season.

In some tropical areas there is a marked wet-dry cycle corresponding to the winter and summer of the temperate zone. Apparently some *Polistes* wasps in these places stop breeding during the dry season and may undergo a sort of quiescence—a period of reduced activity resembling the hibernation of temperate wasps. Phil Rau, who observed tropical *Polistes* colonies in Panama and Mexico, pointed out that this may have been an important preadaptation to life in the temperate zone for a genus probably tropical in origin.

All of the colonies in a temperate-zone *Polistes* population begin and cease nesting at about the same times of year. However some equatorial populations of *Polistes* have very little if any seasonal synchrony of colony cycles; nests are being founded at all times of the year and colonies of all stages are found in all seasons. What controls the colony cycle in such a population—why are nests not inhabited forever? Field observations suggest that the length of the colony cycle depends on the reproductive longevity of the queen. The first sign of a declining *Polistes* colony—one soon to be abandoned by the resident adults—is the cessation of egg-laying. In the temperate zone this is presumably the result of an environmentally induced reproductive arrest preventing the production of young unable to mature before the onset of winter; but in the continuously nesting tropical wasps it awaits the disappearance, incapacity, or senility of the individual queen —an event occurring at different times in different colonies.

With the decline of a colony new nests are founded by the defunct queen's offspring. In *P. canadensis* it is common to find several tiny newly-founded nests near a waning colony, each attended by from one to ten or eleven sisters who regularly visit the parental nest to solicit food. Dominance conflict is frequent among associating foundresses, and fighting sometimes results in the usurpation of a foundress queen's position by a newcomer. But there is always only one egg-laying female on each nest.

The way in which colony multiplication occurs in one tropical species is illustrated by the history of a colony of *P. canadensis* observed in Colombia. After producing a large brood and numerous workers and non-worker females, the queen was experimentally removed from the nest. Soon empty cells began to appear and three of her non-worker daughters began to fight, chasing each other and the workers from the nest. The brood declined, larvae and eggs shriveled and became discolored, apparently due to neglect. Eventually two of the contending daughters left to found nests independently nearby; the third daughter, who dominated the others during the weeks of conflict following the removal of their mother, oviposited and initiated cells on the old nest, in effect starting a new colony there. By this time the former staff of workers had disappeared, having been repeatedly chased from the nest by the aggressive contenders. But newly-emerging females—sisters of the new queen—foraged and cared for the new brood. A "record" of these events is discernible in the structure of the nest: the rows of relatively shallow (new) cells initiated by the new queen contrast with the area of deep cells initiated by the original queen and enlarged for a time after her removal. Such a configuration is common on nests found in nature, suggesting that queen succession of this kind may be a regular occurrence.

v . *Other Social Wasps*

There are 30 described genera of social wasps. All but one of them (*Vespula*) have species with all or part of their ranges in the tropics. The Dutch hymenopterist van der Vecht has examined what is known about the geographic distribution of social vespids, and concludes that they probably originated in tropical Asia and Africa, spreading from there into temperate South Africa, Australia, and through temperate Eurasia and North America to tropical Central and South America.

The Stenogastrinae (*Stenogaster* and *Parischnogaster*), although classified in the family Vespidae along with the social wasps, have so far proven to be subsocial wasps, in many respects intermediate between the solitary eumenids and the social vespids. Iwata has described them as "rather dull and depressed wasps that live mostly in gloomy and wet habitats especially along mountain torrents and cascades." As in the eumenids *Synagris* and *Zethus,* a single female builds a cluster of cells, either of mud or of mud mixed with vegetable material, and places an egg loose in the bottom of each cell (rather than glued to the cell wall as in social vespids). The eggs of the Stenogastrinae are intermediate in average size between those of solitary wasps and the relatively small ones produced by social wasps. A food ball of viscid liquid, perhaps regurgitated from the mother's gut, is placed in the cell before the egg hatches. Later the larva is like a young social wasp in that it is progressively fed masticated insects and

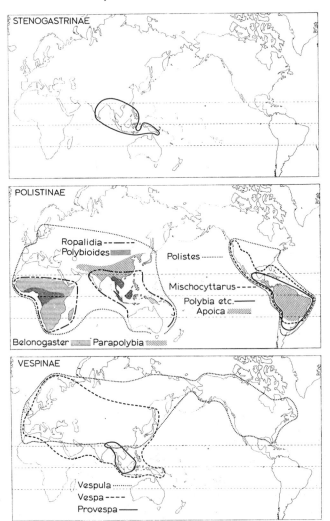

FIG. 89. The geographic distribution of the social wasps. The line for *Polybia* indicates the approximate distribution of various other South American genera, e.g., *Pseudopolybia, Stelopolybia, Chartergus,* and *Epipona.* Only *Brachygastra* lives further north (to ±32° N. latitude). (From van der Vecht, 1967).

spiders. But unlike most social species the mother seals the cell of the mature larva and no cocoon is spun. The female generally attends several cells of various ages simultaneously, and is evidently sometimes still present when her first offspring emerge. Sometimes two or more females are found on the same cluster of cells, but nothing is known of their origins and activities. There is some evidence that offspring females sometimes remain near the parental cells and reuse them or build adjacent new ones. Unfortunately these oriental wasps have not received the study they deserve.

The Polistinae show great diversity in structure of both nests and social organization, but insofar as is known all are social in the sense that females cooperate in brood care. Colonies range in size from those of *Polistes goeldii* in which a single female constructs a nest rarely containing more than 30 cells (there are probably species having a smaller average nest size, but published information on them is unavailable), to those of certain *Polybia* species in which a swarm of more than 3000 females including several queens may start a nest ultimately containing many thousands of cells. Some genera, e.g., the African wasp *Belonogaster* and the many South American species of *Mischocyttarus*, have nests and societies very much like those of *Polistes* described in Chapter IV. In others, e.g., *Protopolybia* and *Stelopolybia*, nests of some species are attended by large numbers of permanently sterile workers morphologically distinguishable from the queens. Of the twenty-five presently recognized genera of Polistinae one (*Polistes*) is cosmopolitan in distribution, and four (*Ropalidia, Belonogaster, Parapolybia* and *Polybioides*) are found only in the Old World tropics. The remaining 20 genera (about 126 species) have ranges centered in tropical South and Central America, leading the British entomologist O.W. Richards to call the American tropics the "metropolis of social wasps."

The subfamily Vespinae consists of three genera (*Vespa, Provespa,* and *Vespula*) of paper wasps having large numbers of sterile workers more or less morphologically distinct from the queens. This group includes the yellow jackets and hornets of temperate North America and Europe. Superficially, they are like *Polistes* gone a step further in the complexity of their social lives. They have large colonies, usually containing several thousand adults and only one queen; they build large enveloped nests having several discoid combs arranged in tiers, like a series of horizontal *Polistes* nests connected by one or several pedicels; and the most obvious differences between the castes are in size and color of females produced at different phases of the colony cycle, as in the temperate *Polistes* species, but with fewer intergrades. But this similarity is somewhat misleading, for the Vespinae constitute a group so distinct morphologically that their phylogenetic relationship with the Polistinae and other vespoid wasps is not clear. It is quite likely that future studies of the many virtually unknown species of the Asian tropics will reveal vespine societies quite different from the North Temperate ones now considered "typical" of the subfamily.

Yellow Jackets and Hornets

To most readers of this book the yellow jackets and hornets (Vespinae) are, along with *Polistes,* the most familiar social wasps. So it seems fitting to present a short resumé of their natural history before discussing special aspects of their biology along with those of other vespids.

In the temperate zone (the habits of the many tropical species are virtually unstudied) colonies are always started by a lone queen which, like a *Polistes* foundress, has mated the previous autumn and passed the winter in a torpid state. Unlike *Polistes* queens, the vespine queens overwinter singly rather than in clusters; and in most species foundress associations are virtually unknown. The queen forages, builds, and cares for a small brood until the first worker females emerge. Then she specializes in egg-laying and rarely leaves the nest.

The nest begins as a single horizontal comb supported by a central pedicel. When it contains only a few shallow cells it is already partially surrounded by an envelope, which begins as an umbrellalike roof, later extended to form a spherical envelope open only at the bottom. As the first comb is enlarged and others are suspended below it, the envelope is repeatedly torn down and rebuilt, a small part at a time, to accommodate the growing colony. At the end of the season a nest usually consists of several combs surrounded by a multilayered envelope, and is attended by several hundred workers and one queen. Underground nests like those shown in Figure 97 are nearly identical in structure to aerial nests of other vespine species.

In most respects the brood-care activities of yellow jackets and hornets are like those of *Polistes*. Workers forage and feed larvae, imbibe fluid exuded by larvae, and cool the nest with water and fanning. Their diet seems somewhat more varied than that of *Polistes*, however, including more dead and decaying material and a greater variety of insects.

Males and large females (future queens) are produced late in the nesting season. In some species the large females are reared in extra large cells constructed in late summer. They mate and overwinter and found nests the following spring. Very little is known about the mating behavior of vespine wasps. In the temperate zone it probably occurs away from the nest. Males do not survive the winter. In most species nests are abandoned at the end of the nesting season and are generally not reused the next year.

Nest Architecture

Most social wasps are known to students of behavior only as dried museum specimens said to have come from a certain remote place and to have built a particular kind of nest. But these bits of information are tantalizing, for, although the amount of morphological variation among the vespids is small compared to that found in most other families of insects, the diversity of nest forms is very great indeed. Since a wasp's nest is a record of complex behavior, this indicates that the Vespidae have diversified behaviorally rather than morphologically; and it seems quite probable that this behavioral diversity extends in some degree to the social organization of the nests' inhabitants.

Virtually all of the social wasps build cells of vegetable fibers. There are a few exceptions among the Central and South American wasps of the genus *Polybia,* the most frequently noted being *Polybia emaciata* whose thin nest envelope and delicately sculptured cells consist entirely of mud. Some of the primitively social Stenogastrinae build nests of mud, and some of a mixture of mud and vegetable particles, as do some solitary wasps (Eumenidae: Zethinae).

Nests of the same type as those of *Polistes*—consisting of a single comb, attached to a support by one or more pedicels, and lacking an envelope—are found in several genera, suggesting that this is a relatively "primitive" nest form. The simplest polistine nest is that of *P. goeldii,* in which the original cell is attached to a single pedicel and the nest enlarged by adding cells in a long series, each new cell being attached by its base to the distal rim of the cell above (Fig. 77a). Similar nests are constructed by species of *Ropalidia, Parapolybia,* and *Mischocyttarus.* The cells are circular in cross-section, and are probably derived from the cylindrical cells built by some mud daubers, perhaps via an intermediate stage in which cells were attached individually to hanging rootlets or plant stems (as in some Stenogastrinae), then to a substrate by a pedicel, then to each other in a series originating on a pedicel (thus economizing in the construction of pedicels). The pedicel may have evolved as an aid to defense against pedestrian predators such as ants; in fact, the junior author of this book has observed *Polistes* workers fending off ants one by one as they traversed this narrow bridge to the nest. This interpretation of the function of the nest pedicel is supported by some recent observations of *Mischocyttarus drewseni* by Robert Jeanne in Brazil. *M. drewseni* builds an unenveloped comb supported by a very long thin pedicel which the wasps frequently rub with the undersides of their abdomens (Fig. 94). Jeanne noticed this and, knowing of a patch of secretory cells on the underside of the final abdominal segment, hypothesized that some secretion is applied by the wasps to the pedicel. He rubbed the secretory area on artificial glass pedicels leading to a "bait" of nutmeats and found that ants traversing the glass pedicels hesitated and often turned back when they encountered a rubbed area, whereas their behavior was unaffected by various other substances applied to the glass. He concluded that material produced by the abdominal gland serves as an "ant repellent" in this species and perhaps in others (e.g., *Polistes canadensis*) having similar nests, glands, and behavior patterns. Similarly, *Leipomeles* females apparently coat the stems of leaves on which their nests are built with a sticky substance said to function as an "ant guard."

In *Ropalidia, Mischocyttarus,* and *Polistes* the construction of horizontal nests with a central pedicel and, sometimes (e.g., in *Polistes fuscatus*), peripheral auxiliary pedicels is often associated with nesting in cavities, whereas the long, pendant vertical nests (e.g., of *Polistes canadensis*) are more often found in the open, beneath leaves and branches, or overhanging rocks. The horizontal nests fit better into shallow crevices and are enlarged asymmetrically to fit the contours of an irregularly shaped attachment surface. Horizontal nests and cavity dwelling predominate in primarily temperate *Polistes* species, suggesting that this nest form may help them survive harsh winters, perhaps because it permits wasps to nest in favorable hibernation sites.

The majority of social wasps build an envelope around the comb (or combs) or cells, and the adult wasps leave and enter the nest via one or a few openings in the envelope. It is common to find alert females stationed at these openings, and the nest envelope, like the pedicel of a naked comb, probably affords protection from parasites and predators by providing restricted access to the brood-containing cells within. In some recent and still unpublished studies of social wasps in Brazil, Robert Jeanne of Harvard University has discovered that bats are important predators of certain *Polybia* species. The bats chew through the paper nest envelope and systematically eat the larvae, returning the next night if one night's pillaging leaves any survivors. Jeanne hypothesizes that some wasps (e.g., *Chartergus* species) are protected from the attacks of bats by having very tough cardboardlike nest envelopes.

Many (perhaps all) paper-making wasps have glands in the head which are sometimes referred to as "glands of construction" because they produce a fluid which apparently acts as the "sizing," or adherent, in the preparation of nest carton from fibers and water. It is probably this same fluid that is applied to the pedicel and top of naked combs, where it dries to form to a hard, shiny lacquerlike coating serving to anchor and waterproof the nest. This substance appears in various amounts in the nest envelopes of different species. In *Metapolybia pediculata* it forms transparent, micalike specks in the envelope, which Phil Rau called "windows" in his description of nests of this species he found in Panama. Various entomologists who have observed the flat "one-story" nests of *Metapolybia* in nature record that this substance gives the nests a mottled cover which, like military camouflage, makes them hard to see against the lichen-covered rocks and trees where they are often found. Wasps of another genus (*Leipomeles*) actually incorporate fragments of lichen into the nest envelope, with the same result, and *Parachartergus fulgidipennis* puts a covering of chewed moss fragments over its envelope producing a green color like the leaf on which it is found.

The nest envelope probably serves various other functions in addition to camouflage. It certainly shields the brood from direct sunlight, wind and rain; and the insulation of the multilayered envelope of such genera as *Vespula* and *Polybia* may increase the effectiveness of temperature regulation. The enveloped nests of *Polybia scutellaris* serve as hibernacula in southern Brazil, where the perennial colonies of this species are exposed to mild winters at the edge of the south temperate zone. As we have already noted, the annually-constructed enveloped nests of the north-temperate Vespinae are evidently not normally used in this way, but are usually abandoned before the onset of cold weather.

The internal structure of enveloped nests is almost as varied as can be imagined, given the general vespid practice of placing cells together to form combs. In some nests (e.g., of the Vespinae) the combs are attached to a support by one or more pedicels, and an envelope is built around but not touching them, so that the nest is like one or more *Polistes* combs enclosed in an envelope. In a few (*Metapolybia, Clypearia, Synoeca* spp.) the cells are placed directly on the substrate, without intervening pedicels. And in other species the envelope becomes the "backing" for cells built directly on it, or serves as the attachment surface for combs with pedicels. The combs of mature nests may form a broad spiral (*Polybioides raphigastra, Protopolybia pumila*), concentric vertical cylinders (*Stelopolybia angulata*), spheres (*Stelopolybia flavipennis*), horizontal tiers (*Stelopolybia vicina* and Vespinae), parallel vertical panels (*Polybioides* spp.), and a variety of less easily described configurations. One of the com-

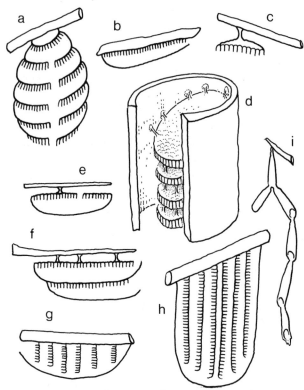

FIG. 90. Diversity in the nest architecture of social wasps. Diagrams show cross-sections representing the general form of the nests of: *a, Polybia, Brachygastra, Epipona, Chartergus, Protonectarina,* and *Synecoides* species; *b, Metapolybia, Clypearia,* and *Synoeca* species; *c, Polistes, Ropalidia, Belonogaster,* and *Mischocyttarus* species; *d, Stelopolybia (Gymnopolybia)* species (cutaway view of combs suspended in a cavity; nest lacks an envelope); *e, Charterginus* species; *f, Protopolybia* species; *g, Parachartergus* species; *h, Polybioides* species; *i, Mischocyttarus punctatus.* (a-h, after Richards and Richards, 1951; i, after a photograph by R.L. Jeanne).

monest architectural styles is that of the large genus *Po-lybia* (also found somewhat modified in *Brachygastra, Chartergus, Epipona, Protonectarina,* and *Synecoides*). The mature nests usually have several combs arranged

FIG. 90A. Longitudinal section through the center of a nest of *Chartergus* (probably *C. chartarius*). The nest measured more than 50 cm. (about 20 inches) in length. Its outward appearance is as shown in Figure 95A. (Photograph by W. D. Hamilton).

one above the other, all of them without pedicels and each with the entire perimeter attached to the envelope. The wasps begin these nests by constructing a domed roof, often placed so that it is tangential to the limb of a tree. A discoid platform is then broadly attached beneath the roof, and the first cells are constructed using the disc as a base. The roof is then extended to form the sides and bottom of the envelope; and the nest is enlarged by building cells on the underside of the floor to form a new comb,

FIG. 91. Nest of a species of *Stelopolybia*. This extraordinary type of nest, having nearly spherical concentric combs, was unknown until 1969, when William Hamilton carefully excavated and photographed this specimen in Brazil.

while the sides are again extended and at the bottom closed. Access to the combs is usually via a hole left in the center of each, in line with the single nest entrance at the nest's bottom. Many of these nests look from the outside like the familiar hornets' nests of Europe and North America. But they are enlarged with more economy of labor, since, unlike the hornets, females of at least some species having nests of this type do not repeatedly tear down and rebuild the nest envelope when adding cells.

In some parts of its range the widespread tropical species *Polybia occidentalis* builds a nest envelope with large spiny processes perhaps acting to protect the colony from large predators seeking the brood or honey stored within. Whatever the function of the spines, they have led the Guarani Indians of Paraguay to distinguish between two similar classes of wasps inhabiting the same area: the "Kavichui," wasps with smooth nests, and the "Kamuati," wasps with spiny nests. These wasps are so similar structurally that early taxonomists called them one variety (*scutellaris*) of *P. occidentalis*. But the differences in nest structure led O.W. Richards to take a closer look at the situation. In 1951 he hypothesized that there are probably two species involved, one building a smooth nest, and the other adding spines to the envelope of relatively old nests. Although the matter is not yet entirely settled, this example illustrates both the value and limitations in the use of nest structure in taxonomy: the nests are easily observed and often lead to the discovery of biological differences not readily evident from pinned specimens alone. But not all nest characters are useful in this way, as they may, like individual morphology, change with age or vary from individual to individual. Thus, in their diagnosis of *P. occidentalis* the Indians were in a sense ahead of the early taxonomists; but they would sometimes have called one species by two different names because of their reliance on a single changing feature of the nest. Comparative nest structure was used extensively by the pioneer Brazilian hymenopterist Adolpho Ducke to construct a phylogeny of the social wasps during the early 1900s. Nests are still deemed useful in this way if considered together with the natural history and structure of their builders.

The Foundation and Longevity of Colonies

Nest founding by social wasps may be either solitary (with the nest initiated and attended by a lone female until her progeny begin to emerge) or social, with more than one female cooperating in these activities. The mode of nest founding may vary within species, as it does in *Polistes,* but generally a particular pattern is characteristic of a given species. The temperate-zone species of *Vespa* and *Vespula* are the only social wasps known to have obligatory solitary nest founding. Until the first offspring adults emerge, the solitary *Vespula* queen forages, cares for the brood, and defends the nest, rearing single-handed the first small brood of workers. Later in the colony cycle she becomes an egg-laying specialist; in some *Vespa* species she is eventually incapable of flight, presumably because of the weight of her egg-laden ovaries.

New colonies of *Mischocyttarus* and *Belonogaster,* like those of *Polistes,* are also sometimes founded by a solitary queen. But frequently in these genera the nest initiator is joined by one or more other females. This form of social nest founding, in which the foundress females arrive at the site of a newly-started nest one by one rather than as a group, is sometimes called "association" to distinguish it from "swarming," in which the foundress group forms at the parental nest and moves *en masse* to a new nest site. The only time females of these genera are known to start a new colony with a large initial group of females is in cases of destruction of the parental nest, when a large group of residents frequently builds a new nest on or near the site of the one that was destroyed.

True swarming is evidently common in the tropical Polistinae, as indicated by the occurrence of newly-founded nests, having many cells either containing very young brood or still empty, attended by a large group of adults, and located an appreciable distance from other nests of the same species. There is good evidence of swarming in

FIG. 92. Swarm of a species of *Clypearia* and a newly-founded nest. The cells are flush against the substrate on which the nest was built, the envelope only partially completed. Bright drops of nectar are visible in some cells. Nest structure is as shown in Figure 90b. (Photograph by R.L. Jeanne).

nine genera: *Apoica, Brachygastra, Synoeca, Polybia, Angiopolybia, Metapolybia, Stelopolybia, Protopolybia,* and *Parachartergus.* Swarming is considered the most likely mode of nest founding in the ten genera of social wasps whose early colony history is completely unknown. In general the swarming species have large, often perennial colonies, and the swarms are seasonal. The swarms commonly build a large number of cells in a few days, and eggs appear only after the nest structure is well established. This rapid initial construction of the nest is often followed by a lull in which little expansion of the structure occurs.

The order of business for an active swarm varies from species to species: some (*Angiopolybia* sp.) complete the nest envelope first, leaving room for future expansion of the initial comb; in *Metapolybia* the order is cell building–oviposition–envelope construction; in *Polybia* and *Synoeca* the swarm works on the comb and envelope at the same time followed by oviposition later (at least in *Po-*

lybia). Phil Rau observed the behavior of a swarm of *Metapolybia pediculata* containing about thirty individuals. First they rested idly on a slanting timber for about four days. Then there was a "stir" in the center of the group, and foragers began coming and going to and from the spot, establishing within a few hours a nucleus of ten cells. After four days of building, and shortly before the completion of the comb, the first eggs appeared in the cells; and four days later the wasps began a wall around the edges of the comb, the beginning of an envelope completed fifteen days after initiation of building activity. The annual nests of *M. pediculata* are evidently completed in this initial burst of building activity.

Swarms of *Polybia scutellaris* have been observed in Brazil and in Argentina. In southern Brazil swarming occurs during the rainy season. The first sign that swarming is about to occur is a "stirring" on a mature nest. Then an aggregation of adults appears and grows over a period of two to six days. Evidence that swarming *Polybia* wasps move *en masse* to the new nest site was provided by the observation of one group of over three hundred individuals in a temporary resting place, unassociated with any nest. When the swarm settles at the new site it begins construction, making up to four combs (about nine hundred cells) in one or two days. The rainy season also brings out large numbers of flying ants and termites, and after two or three days of uninterrupted building the swarming wasps begin to hunt and capture the winged sexual individuals of these insects. They cut off and discard the heads and all or some of the appendages of their victims and store them in the infant nest, filling pockets found in the multilayered nest envelope. The fate of the stored insect meat is unknown. If it is used a week or so later to feed larvae there must be some way of protecting the booty from infestations and mold during the humid swarming season. Once the provisioning is completed (sometimes during the course of one afternoon) construction activity resumes at an accelerated pace. One swarm took only ten days to complete a nest about a foot in diameter and containing ten combs. All of this takes place before any eggs are laid, in contrast to the situation described in the previous chapter on *Polistes*, in which there is a close temporal (and physiological) association between cell-addition and oviposition.

It is interesting to speculate about the function of swarming. The most striking known consequence of this behavior is the rapid establishment of a nest. But why are so many tropical wasps, living in an area where nesting is possible throughout the year, in such a hurry to complete a nest? Perhaps such behavior affords protection against predators and parasites likely to attack a brood left exposed in unenveloped combs, or unguarded by workers preoccupied with building. So few swarms have been observed that it is perhaps impossible at this time to appreciate some of the selective advantages of this mode of nest founding. Nothing is known about what triggers swarming, how new nesting sites are selected, what coordinates the movement by many individuals to a new site, or what stimulates building behavior in a waiting swarm. Dissections of females inhabiting newly founded nests have revealed the presence of more than one fertilized female with developed ovaries, suggesting that some swarms may contain more than one queen, and direct observations of oviposition by marked wasps confirm the existence of multiple-queen colonies.

Early students of social wasps assumed that tropical colonies are characteristically perennial and multiply by swarming, and that temperate-zone species are annual and "haplometrotic", or founded by solitary queens. Now the proper generalizations seem to be that all known modes of nest founding occur among the tropical species, with most swarmers (at least some species of *Brachygastra, Synoeca, Polybia, Protopolybia,* and *Epipona*) having perennial colonies, and most solitary-foundress and association-founded colonies usually lasting one year or less (an exception occurs in *Metapolybia,* a tropical wasp which swarms, yet has annual colonies). Neither swarming nor perennial nesting occurs in the temperate zone. Some of the perennial colonies may be very long-lived. Brazilian colonies of *Polybia scutellaris* reportedly last as long as twenty-five years. (One very old nest of *Polybia scutellaris* measured seventy-five centimeters—about thirty inches—in diameter.) There are numerous reports of *Synoeca surinama* colonies being five or six years old and a Brazilian *Synoeca cyanea* nest lasted for sixteen years.

Colony Defense

In an extensive report on the social wasps of South America Drs. O. W. and M. J. Richards include a section on "Methods of taking nests," in which they describe the capture of colonies of a species with the forbidding, and apparently apt, name *Polybia rejecta:*

"The nests were attached 15 ft. from the ground on trees infested with Dolichoderine ants. The wasps were too aggressive for the nest to be approached very closely on a ladder. The method we adopted was to tie a net onto a long pole, and a cutlass onto another. If one person then holds up the net, another can knock the nest into it. . . . The difficulty in this method is to cut off the nest near enough to its point of attachment to the bough and to prevent the escape of wasps between the time the nest falls into the net and the moment when it is possible to tie it up."

Another ingenious method of nest collection is used by some natives of British Guiana to obtain the whitish, tough-cartoned nests of *Chartergus* for sale to Europeans as curios. These men seek out a nest on a branch overhanging a river, carefully ascend the "wasp tree," and sever the branch with one well-directed blow of a machete. The river has a dual function: if the attempt is successful the nest falls into the water and can be retrieved after the wasps leave. If the nest fails to fall the hunter takes to the water instead to evade the infuriated wasps. This kind of human behavior attests to the effectiveness of nest protection by social wasps attacking and stinging *en masse*. But this is only one of a variety of behavior patterns contributing to colony defense.

A prerequisite of defensive behavior is the ability to detect intruders and distinguish friend from foe. *Polistes* wasps evidently recognize an ichneumonid parasite of their brood (described in the previous chapter) by sight, since they react to it only when it moves. The sensitivity of wasps to substrate vibrations has already been mentioned. Often even a slight jarring of the object to which a nest is attached is sufficient to alert an entire colony; in this case the substrate serves as both a detection and a warning system. Observers of *Polistes* and the Vespinae have noted that nestmates come and go freely at the nest whereas "foreign" individuals of the same species are attacked as they approach. In the case of *Polistes* the foreign wasps may be recognized by their more hesitating flight: they often approach in a bobbing, circuitous flight in contrast to homing individuals, which fly in a "beeline" directly to the nest. The *Polistes* females at the nest sometimes attack nestmates which approach sluggishly, either due to inexperience or to being heavily laden with foraged material. When nestmate recognition has no readily apparent explanation, as is often the case, a "colony odor" is often suspected; but as yet there is no direct evidence of chemical recognition cues in any social wasp.

During periods of activity, when many workers are engaged in foraging and brood care, one commonly finds some alert individuals either spaced out on the nest envelope or, in the case of unenveloped nests, on the comb. During periods of inactivity the resting wasps usually adopt positions on the nest making it difficult for an intruder to approach unnoticed. In some social wasps, e.g., *Vespula* species, the adults spend their "sleeping" time inside the nest, some of them with their heads facing out of the single nest entrance. In *Polybia simillima*, on the other hand, many adults spend the night on the outside of the nest where they cover the entire envelope with their bodies "ranged in rows with almost mathematical precision." At night mature nests of *Polistes fuscatus* characteristically have a dense cluster of males and the passive, nonworker females on top of the comb, and the smaller number of workers—the more aggressive females—dispersed on the relatively exposed face of the nest. The nocturnally active wasps of the genus *Apoica* inhabit unenveloped nests with a single central attachment and a thick, cone-shaped top. In daytime the wasps rest on the nest face only, covering the comb with their bodies, and with the peripheral females aligned facing the edge of the nest (Fig. 93). It would thus be very difficult for even a small intruder to reach the brood without touching (and alerting) an adult; and the entire edge of the nest fairly bristles with sensory apparatus—the eyes and antennae of the outward-facing wasps. The thick "roof" of the nest probably affords protection from parasites and predators approaching from above.

In some species substrate vibrations and mass vigilance may be supplemented by chemical alarm signals serving to alert an entire colony to a threat detected by one or a few individuals. Such communicative chemicals, or "pheromones," are known to function in the colony defense of ants and bees. A substance thought to be an alarm pheromone has been discovered among the compounds composing the venom of a species of *Vespa*, but knowledge of its function awaits further investigation.

It is a well known fact that dangerous or distasteful animals, such as poisonous reptiles and certain ill-flavored butterflies (e.g., monarchs), often have striking patterns of behavior or color serving to warn potential attackers. A rattlesnake's rattle is an example. The selective advantage of this is clear: there is a certain probability of injury

FIG. 93. A colony of the nocturnal wasp, *Apoica pallens,* resting in daytime. Note the defensive alignment of wasps at the nest periphery. (Photograph by W. D. Hamilton).

or even death in an encounter with a foe. So even a well-armed animal benefits by giving a conspicuous warning signal and avoiding risky interactions. The most striking example of a warning display known in the social wasps occurs in the tropical American species *Synoeca surinama.* These shiny blue-black wasps build a comb flush against a supporting surface (usually a tree trunk or large branch) and cover it with a single-layered, rather brittle envelope. When undisturbed most of the wasps remain inside the nest, in the ample space between envelope and comb. When disturbed they produce a warning signal by somehow vibrating the nest envelope in unison from within, producing a rhythmic drumming sound audible several yards away. If further aroused hundreds of individuals rush out onto its outer surface, where they continue the coordinated thumping, at the same time raising and lowering their wings in synchrony with the sound so that the nest is suddenly a rhythmically throbbing mass of aroused wasps. Thus the warning is both auditory and visual. *Synoeca surinama* is one of a few species of social wasps with barbed stings, which, like those of honeybees, remain in the wound following an attack. So it is not surprising that these wasps, which may lose part of their body in battle, perform a spectacular warning display when threatened. And it is little wonder that natives of the regions inhabited by these wasps consider it an "outstanding act of valor" to approach their nests.

A number of the other social wasps are especially noted for their aggressiveness, including the South American species *Epipona tatua, Chartergus charterginus,* and various *Polybia* species. Species of the genus *Polybioides* in the old world tropics are not only "extremely pugnacious," but commonly produce colonies containing several thousand individuals. Sir Henry M. Stanley, the pioneer European explorer of tropical Africa, described their colonies as "terror," and booby traps attached to *Polybioides* colonies are among the barbarities of modern warfare in Southeast Asia.

The opposite extreme in defensive behavior is represented by *Protopolybia emortualis,* which rather than becoming aggressive when threatened retires to its nest and leaves the active business of defense to some fierce and numerous tree-nesting ants (*Dolichoderus bidens*). These ants swarm over the leaves and branches of the tree when it is shaken, making it very unpleasant for any intruder. Other social wasps commonly building their nests in trees

FIG. 94. *Mischocyttarus drewseni* female rubbing the nest pedicel with the tip of her abdomen. A secretion produced by a gland on the underside of the abdomen is applied in this fashion, and repels ants approaching the comb via the long pedicel. (Photograph by R.L. Jeanne).

inhabited by Dolichoderine ants are *Polybia rejecta*, *P. lugubris*, *Stelopolybia pallipes*, *Synoeca surinama*, *Synoeca virginea*, and some *Mischocyttarus* species. Birds' nests are also commonly found in the trees housing ants and wasps. Presumably the birds also gain protection from the association. On one tree bearing a *Dolichoderus* nest O. W. and M. J. Richards found no less than eight nests of *Polybia rejecta,* colonies of two different species of *Mischocyttarus,* one colony each of *Protopolybia* and

FIG. 95. Nesting association of a Brazilian social wasp (*Synoeca virginea*) and an ant (*Azteca sp.*). The cone-shaped ants' nest (above) was probably built first, the wasps' nest (center) later. (Photograph by W. D. Hamilton).

FIG. 95A. Nesting association of a social wasp (*Chartergus* species, probably *C. chartarius*) and a tropical oriole (*Cacicus cela*). (Photograph by W. D. Hamilton).

Metapolybia, and an oriole nest. *Protopolybia picteti* is another "ant tree" species behaving timidly when approached.

Another type of non-aggressive defensive behavior is found in *Mischocyttarus fitzgeraldi.* The adults fall as if dead when disturbed, then "recover" before hitting the ground and fly away.

Foraging and Brood Care

Most of what wasps do could be listed under the heading "brood care," including building behavior and colony defense. For the cells of the nests are devoted exclusively to housing the young and storage of food for the young; and even the most aggressive of the colony-dwelling wasps are generally no more belligerent than solitary wasps when away from the nest. The importance of the presence of brood is illustrated by the behavior of females of *Metapolybia pediculata* observed in Panama. When the cells are empty these wasps fail to attack even under extreme provocation—they actually run away from a stick poked into the comb. But as soon as the cells contain eggs the workers become aggressive toward intruders.

The information presently available on the behavior of vespids at the nest suggests that their brooding behavior is basically similar to that of *Polistes.* In all of the social species a single offspring occupies each paper cell and the larva progressively receives food, in the form of masticated flesh of insects or other arthropods, from the adult females. With the exception of the provisioning described above by *Polybia* in newly-founded nests, the social wasps generally do not store their proteinaceous provisions in the nest, so it is difficult to assess the variety or specificity of arthropods captured by a given species. Usually when a close study of the larval diet has been made (for example, in some species of *Polistes, Vespula,* and *Stenogaster*) it has proven to consist of a variety of different adult and immature arthropods, and to change with the changing abundance of prey species. In good weather at the end of the season, the workers of a mature colony of *Vespula vulgaris* bring three to four thousand prey loads to the nest each day, the booty consisting mostly of spiders, flies, and assorted insect larvae. This illustrates the importance of a large social wasp colony as a predator of insects and other small arthropods.

Some information on larval diet can be gleaned from observations of hunting wasps. *Polybia occidentalis* catches large numbers of small biting flies which rank with mosquitoes as a nuisance in Paraguay, catching them particularly around the eyes of cows. The larvae of *Belonogaster brevipetiolatus* are evidently fed lepidopterous larvae, as in *Polistes.* But they evidently also receive adult butterflies: the adults of this species have been seen in the field masticating adult butterflies, and the intestinal tracts of some dissected *B. brevipetiolatus* larvae contained butterfly legs. *Belonogaster junceus* preys on orb-weaving spiders. The huntress hovers up and down before the web, approaching it more and more closely and finally touching it lightly without becoming ensnared. This stimulates the spider to move from its retreat at the side of the web to the center, where the wasp plucks it off with its mandibles and forelegs. Some species of *Mischocyttarus, Parischnogaster,* and *Stenogaster* also hunt at spiders' webs, but these wasps rob the webs of prey not used by the spider rather than capturing the spider itself. *Stenogaster varipictus* is especially adept at this, carefully going over the web without touching it, picking out with her mouth and feet the tiny midges and other light insects, and masticating them into a smooth paste which is then fed to her larvae or stored in globules in egg-containing cells. *S. varipictus* is even able to exploit horizontal or inclined webs by hovering and examining them from beneath. *Vespa* females often plunder the nests of various other social wasps, including *Ropalidia* and *Parapolybia,* removing larvae and stored provisions while the relatively tiny inhabitants stand by passively. *Vespa tropica* reportedly preys exclusively on larvae and pupae of various species of *Polistes* and *Parapolybia,* at least in some parts of its range.

Sweet-tasting droplets have been found in the cells of so many different social wasps that it is probably safe to conclude that most, if not all, social species gather and consume honey. Presumably the honey is fed to larvae, although it is difficult to distinguish from water, masticated food, and secretions also transferred mouth-to-mouth between adults and larvae. Like bees, wasps collect nectar from a wide variety of flowering plants. They seem to exploit any available source of concentrated sugar, including man-made sweets, ripe fruits, and honey stored by bees (as mentioned in Chapter I). *Polybia scutellaris, Pseudopolybia compressa, Parachartergus apicalis, Stelopolybia pallipes,* and *Vespula* workers also collect the "honeydew" secreted by certain leafhoppers, aphids, mealybugs, and scale insects.

Foraging social insects are famous for their ability to communicate with each other regarding the location of food sources. The odor trails of some ants and stingless bees, and the "dance language" of honeybees are examples of communication among foragers. There is no evidence that such precise communication occurs in either *Polistes* or *Vespula,* the most frequently studied genera of social wasps. In *Polistes* the return of a forager often causes a rise in activity (grooming, soliciting, attention to larvae, and general movement) on the nest, and this in turn often leads to the flight of workers and thus to an increase in the foraging rate. The colonies in which complex communication is most likely to occur—the large and apparently specialized societies of some of the tropical Polistinae— are presently the least well known. A man who watched a colony of *Polybia atra* on his veranda in Venezuela observed that returning foragers made repeated excited turns among the group of about fifty females usually sitting on the nest envelope. He called this a "Schwänzel- tanz" (waggle dance), thus inviting comparison with the dance of honeybees, and reported that it incited the nest wasps to activity and flight. Later, Martin Lindauer, co-

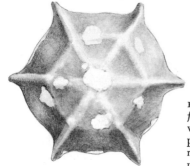

FIG. 96. Nest of *Charterginus fulvus.* The starlike six-sided envelope conforms to the almost perfectly hexagonal comb which results when cells are added sym- metrically about a hexagonal cen- tral cell.

investigator with Karl von Frisch of communication among bees, briefly studied forager recruitment in *Polybia scutellaris*. He found that ten wasps visiting a feeding site 150 meters from their nest "recruited" five to seven new foragers to the site in one half-hour, and concluded from the behavior of the newcomers, which seemed to search rather than orient directly to the area, that precise information regarding the location of the site had not been communicated. However, the "dance language" of *Polybia*, like the honeybee dance, does evidently inform potential foragers of the discovery of a food source. The possibility that the intensity of the dance might correlate with the nearness or richness of the source, and hence might influence the number of foragers arriving at a site, has not been investigated.

The life of a larva in a colony of one of the specialized social wasps is monitored almost minute by minute. Workers of *Vespa orientalis* visit each large (fifth instar) larva an average of seventy-four times an hour. Smaller larvae receive fewer visits, but even the smallest is attended an average of fifty-three times an hour. Furthermore, the large (fifth instar) larvae of this species are evidently able to signal their hunger to attending adults. They rub their mandibles against the cell as soon as they finish ingesting a particle of food, and the resulting sound, which is audible to the human ear, apparently stimulates the workers to bring more food. Younger larvae are unable to produce this sound because they are too small to touch the cell walls with their heads; when an inspecting worker finds such a larva without food it taps the tip of its abdomen against the comb, and this may also serve as a "hunger signal" to food-laden workers.

Another important aspect of brood care, especially for wasps inhabiting enclosed nests, is the removal of wastes and debris from around the combs. The significance of this behavior is presumably the elimination of infestations that might occur if dead organic material were allowed to accumulate in the nest. Workers are often observed coming to the nest entrance and dropping debris particles or dead brood to the ground. In some cases they fly as much as seventy feet to drop the debris away from the nest.

The task of nest sanitation is simplified in most social wasps because the larvae do not defecate, but concentrate solid excreta in the meconium and nitrogenous wastes in the body cavity in the form of uric acid. As explained in Chapter II, the meconium is discharged at the end of larval life, and the uric acid during the first days of adulthood. In all of the New World species of social wasps the discharged meconium remains in the bottom of the cell when the adult emerges, and when cells are reused several times (as they frequently are in the Vespinae and long-lived colonies of the tropical Polistinae), the accumulated meconia may come to occupy a large portion of the cell. The adults compensate for this by lengthening the cell walls. However a different pattern is followed by the Old World Polistinae. In *Ropalidia, Belonogaster, Parapolybia,* and *Polybioides*—all of the exclusively old-world Polistinae —the adult wasps chew a neat hole in the bottom of the cell and remove the larval excrement. They then seal over the hole with a thin, shiny, material resembling the "windows" of a *Metapolybia* nest-envelope, and probably composed of the same kind of secretion (see "Nest Architecture," above). In *Belonogaster* the adults sometimes fail to open the cell of a mature larva, and in these cases the excrement is extruded like spaghetti through breaks in the carton. *Belonogaster* is apparently the only vespid genus in which cells are not reused; vacated cells are torn down by the adults, and the old paper used as pulp in the construction of new cells.

Excess water is also among the undesirable materials removed from nests. The females of a *Polybia scutellaris* colony observed for a month in Brazil routinely ejected water from the nest by coming to the entrance, leaning out with legs quivering, and letting a drop of water fall from the mouth to the ground, often grooming it off with a foreleg. This behavior was most frequent in the morning and on humid days. It occurred at the rate of about twen-

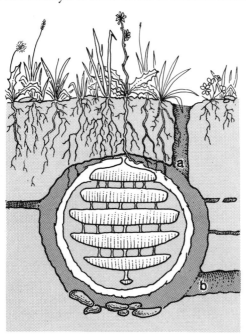

FIG. 97. Subterranean nest of *Vespula germanica*, showing the access tunnel (a) and the burrow of a mole (b) which was enlarged by the wasps to form a nesting cavity. Other small burrows entering the cavity have been closed off by the wasps; stones too heavy to carry out have fallen to the bottom of the cavity during excavation. The nest is suspended from roots at the top of the cavity. This type of architecture—several horizontal combs connected by pedicels and surrounded by an envelope attached only at the top—characterizes both subterranean and aerial nests of all Vespinae (yellow jackets and hornets). (After Janet, 1895).

ty-five drops per hour even though the nest did not appear wet, suggesting that the wasps squeeze water from damp carton with their mandibles. After a heavy rainfall these wasps even "bailed out" some leaves holding rainwater threatening to inundate the nest. They also chewed away leaves overhanging the nest where water collected and dripped onto the envelope.

Water transport and fanning as a means of temperature regulation have been mentioned in the chapter on *Polistes*. This method of cooling the nest is also found in the Vespinae. During prolonged hot spells *Vespula media* workers chew supplementary ventilation holes in the nest envelope. Fanning wasps appear at these holes, which are closed when the weather becomes cooler. A study of *Vespula vulgaris* in Germany revealed that temperature regulation in the enveloped underground colonies of this wasp rivals that of bees (Fig. 98). It is well known that honeybees maintain a constant temperature in the hive, and even keep warm during winter, using metabolic heat generated by buzzing their wings. The German biologist A. Himmer showed that the body temperature of a *Polistes* female can rise to 3 C° above the air temperature during prolonged fanning, and in *V. vulgaris* a fanning female's temperature can rise from 6 to 10.5 C°. In the unenveloped *Polistes* nest such heat is not sufficient to warm the nest appreciably; but a colony of 800-1500 individuals of *V. vulgaris* can hold the temperature nearly constant in spite of a widely fluctuating environmental temperature. During one week when the outdoor temperature varied

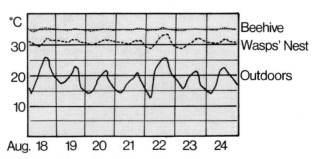

FIG. 98. Regulation of the temperature in a nest of *Vespa vulgaris* (see Figure 97). Constancy of the temperature in the wasps' nest approaches that in a beehive despite wide fluctuations in environmental temperature. (After Himmer, 1932).

between 9°C. and 34°C. (about 48°F. and 91.5°F.) the temperature inside the nest varied only 2.5C.° (between 29.5°C. and 32°C.). Temperature regulation has never been studied in tropical social wasps, but some scattered behavioral observations suggest that it occurs. In Venezuela *Polybia atra* puts drops of water on the nest envelope on hot days; and fanning at the nest entrance has been observed in *Polybia scutellaris* females in Brazil.

Division of Labor and Castes

The "social" insects differ from the "solitary" species in having cooperative brood care. That is, the adults nest in groups in which the activities of at least some of the individuals benefit the offspring of one or more others. It is possible to conceive of a social group in which each female both lays eggs and cares for the young, in indiscriminately guarding and feeding both her own offspring and those of other members of the group. But in fact no such society is yet known among the insects. Instead, insect societies characteristically have a division of labor, with individuals more or less specialized for the performance of certain tasks. The primary division of labor is between reproductive and non-reproductive (or less reproductive) individuals. In some social insects there is a further division of labor within the non-reproductive (worker) caste, with individuals of a certain age or structure specializing as foragers, guards, or nurses.

Understanding the origin and evolution of insect social behavior amounts to understanding the origin and evolution of the division of labor. So this aspect of the natural history of wasps is of fundamental interest, and is much discussed in writings on the biology of the social insects. It is therefore embarrassing to have to admit that we know almost nothing about the nature of the division of labor in most genera of social wasps. This is because the only way to ascertain which tasks are performed by which females is to watch the day-to-day activities of identifiable (marked) individuals; and simple observation is not a popular technique, even among students of behavior. Most of what we can say about the subject is in the form of educated guesses based on studies of colonies whose division of labor has been carefully eliminated in killing jars to facilitate dissections and structural measurements.

The social Hymenoptera (wasps, ants, and bees) differ from the other major group of social insects, the Isoptera (termites) in having exclusively female societies. When males are present in hymenopteran colonies they contribute little or nothing to brood care, and their primary function, mating, is often discharged at aggregations away from the nest (see Chapter IV). In all of the wasps in which mature colonies have been directly and frequently observed (various species of *Polistes, Vespula,* and *Vespa*) there is only one ovipositing female, or queen. Only in exceptional conditions, for example, when the queen disappears from a colony, or during the period of queen determination in *Polistes* (see Chapter IV) or toward the end of the season in the Vespinae (when workers may contribute numerous male-producing eggs), do other females lay eggs. However, there is considerable indirect evidence of multiple queens in other social wasps.

In a "whirlwind" two-month study of social wasps in British Guiana, O.W. and M.J. Richards collected several hundred entire colonies, carefully noting if any individuals escaped capture. They dissected thousands of these wasps in order to determine the degree of development of their ovaries, and from this information obtained an estimate of the number of queens and workers in each colony. A "queen" in the Richards' study was a female having mature eggs in her ovary and sperm in her spermatheca—a mated female in egg-laying condition. A "worker" was an unmated female with undeveloped ovaries. Unmated females were classed as "intermediates" if they had somewhat developed ovaries. Of seven genera with representative species studied in this way, only one, *Mischocyttarus,*

FIG. 99. Difference in size of ovaries of a queen (left) and a worker (right) wasp (*Polistes fuscatus*), used to distinguish probable caste of dissected females.

proved to have only one queen per colony. The other six genera had multiple queens in some or all colonies examined. In *Polybia, Metapolybia, Parachartergus,* and *Stelopolybia fulvo-fasciatus* the ovaries of the "queens" were distinctly larger than those of the "workers" and there were few intermediates; in *Brachygastra, Protopolybia,* and *Stelopolybia pallens,* on the other hand, there were many intermediates whose ovaries varied from workerlike to queenlike, making it difficult to distinguish probable queens from probable workers on the basis of ovary size.

Further evidence that there may sometimes be more than one queen per colony, at least in newly founded nests, is provided by the Richards' observation that a large number of eggs can be produced in a short time. In one *Polybia* nest, for example, 167 eggs were laid in two days. It is very unlikely that this number could be deposited by a single female, since queens on newly-founded *Polybia* nests usually have only five to seven mature eggs in the ovary at a time. Dissection of the swarm that founded the nest showed that twenty-two females had developed ovaries. If all of these females were laying eggs they would each have contributed an average of only 3.8 eggs per day, a figure well within the realm of possibility for young

Polybia queens. Richards and Richards consider multiple queens a secondary development in the evolution of wasp societies, which probably originally contained only one queen. Having multiple queens may, like swarming, be a device for rapid establishment of a large colony.

The wasps of the genus *Belonogaster* have long been considered the most primitively social of the Polistinae. They were studied in the early 1900s by a French scientist named Etienne Roubaud, who went to the Congo with an expedition to study sleeping sickness and became interested in the behavior of the solitary and social wasps of the region. From Roubaud's descriptions the social organization of *Belonogaster* appears to be much like that of *Polistes canadensis:* a single female begins a nest, and is often joined shortly thereafter by one or more other females. In at least some cases the six to seven associated foundresses are from the same parental nest, and visit it to obtain pulp and food. Colonies of all stages were found year around, indicating that there is no marked seasonal synchrony of colony cycles. Some foundresses, and all newly-emerged females function as workers; as in *Polistes,* only the egg-laying females initiate cells. Roubaud thought that no "true workers" exist in *Belonogaster* because dissections showed that all foundresses have developed ovaries, and nest growth of new colonies is proportional to the number of foundresses present; thus, he reasoned, all females must be capable of laying eggs, and all must be initiating cells (a prerogative of egg-layers). However, it is possible for non-ovipositing foundresses to have developed ovaries, as in *P. canadensis;* and by foraging and supplying the queen with pulp, worker foundresses can indirectly contribute to the rate of new cell addition without initiating cells themselves. Thus it may be wrong to conclude from Roubaud's observations that there are no non-reproductive females in *Belonogaster*. Still, *Belonogaster* ranks among the most primitively social wasps in having a small number of workers per colony and very slight differences between castes.

Caste distinctions generally become more and more marked as the colony ages. In the Vespinae, as already pointed out, the solitary queen functions as both reproductive and worker until her daughters begin to forage and care for the brood. Then she forages less or not at all and may even become incapable of flight. Richards and Richards report that in large tropical colonies of *Polybia,* queens which have evidently been laying for a long time can sometimes be identified by sight because they have swollen abdomens. Their dissections indicated that this is due to abdominal distension by the large ovaries, which in the queens become increasingly developed with age: in *Protopolybia minutissima,* for example, queens of a newly founded colony had five to seven ripe eggs whereas those on older nests had twelve to sixteen mature eggs each.

So far we have discussed only behavioral differences between queens and workers, and morphological differences that result from these behavioral differences during the adult lifetime of the individual. What about caste distinctions apparent in the newly-emerged adults? Such differences are well known in ants and termites, in which the reproductive adults are winged and often very different in appearance from the workers; and honeybee queens are considerably larger than workers at the time of emergence. The most marked caste differences in size now known among the social wasps are found in the Vespinae —the hornets and yellow jackets. In these wasps the queens are generally much larger than the workers. In temperate-zone species the large females are produced late in the colony cycle, and the size dimorphism is thought to be due to a seasonal increase in the amount of food given to larvae. The ratio of workers (food-getters) to larvae increases as the season advances and; in some species the queens are raised in large cells constructed to-

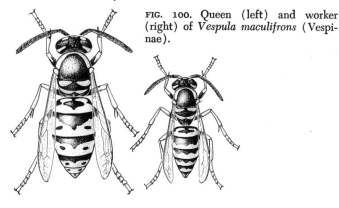

FIG. 100. Queen (left) and worker (right) of *Vespula maculifrons* (Vespinae).

ward the end of the colony cycle. The large cells may stimulate workers to increase the amount of food given to the larvae inhabiting them; they do not directly affect the size of the larva, since queen-size individuals occasionally emerge from small cells. Emerging queens are also somewhat larger than workers in *Polybia scutellaris* and *Stelopolybia vicina*, both tropical American species.

Structural differences between queens and workers have been found in three genera of social wasps: *Protopolybia* (two species), *Stelopolybia* (one species), and *Polybia* (four species). A recurrent queen characteristic in these species is a wider base of the abdomen, a character that many be related in some way to the accomodation of large ovaries in queens. Such differences are often accompanied by differences in size, and must arise in the pre-adult developmental stages, for structural features of wasps do not change after emergence from the cocoon. Structural caste dimorphism in *Stelopolybia flavipennis* was studied by W.D. Hamilton in Brazil. Queens and workers are so obviously different in this species (Fig. 101) that students of museum collections have sometimes treated them as separate species.

Most discussions of "caste determination" in social wasps and other social insects are concerned with the

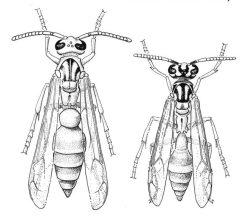

FIG. 101. Queen (left) and worker (right) of *Stelopolybia flavipennis* (Polistinae), showing size and structural differences between the castes.

causes of these size and morphological caste characteristics. As we have already mentioned, quantitative differences in diet between queen and worker larvae probably account for size differences between the castes; they may also explain structural differences if, as in the ants, these differences are "allometric", or size-dependent. The causes of behavioral differences may or may not prove to be the same, and are more difficult to study in the laboratory. Other possible mechanisms of caste determination have been suggested by analogy with other insects. They include qualitative differences in food or secretions received by larvae, differences in the kind or amount of material included in the egg when it is laid, and developmental differences triggered by seasonal changes in environmental temperature or photoperiod.

Since structural differences between vespid queens and workers are unusual, and small when they exist, it is not surprising that there is no known example of structural differentiation among the workers of a colony. Perhaps the closest approach to this is in late-summer nests of *Vespula*, where some workers seem to specialize in brood care and others in foraging. Some observers have the impression that relatively small workers produced early in the season predominate among the nurses, whereas larger workers are foraging specialists.

Aside from this one possible case, even behavioral sub-castes among workers are unknown in the social wasps. However, in *Polistes* and *Vespula* individuals tend to persist in a given task on a given day. This temporary specialization is due at least in part to the ability of wasps to learn. Females return time after time to the same food, pulp, or water source, initially performing orientation flights over it before leaving as when first learning a nest site. Then, when the source is exhausted, they "forget" that site and move on to another place or a different task. This ability to return to proven sites of course contributes to foraging efficiency by greatly reducing the time and energy expended in hunting. The efficiency of foragers is further increased at the nest, where nestmates take and distribute all or part of the load brought in, thus freeing the experienced forager for another trip. This procedure is apparently more common in some species than in others. *Polistes* workers returning with pulp usually apply it to the nest themselves, except when solicited from by the queen. However, in *Polybia scutellaris* and *Metapolybia pediculata,* nest wasps take the pulp at the nest entrance and the forager immediately leaves on another foraging trip.

In general, then, a social wasp worker seems to be a non-ovipositing Jack-of-all-trades capable of changing her specialty from one minute to the next regardless of her size or age. In the few species in which she differs in appearance from the queen the distinctions between the two castes are slight.

The Evolution of Social Behavior in Wasps

We left the solitary wasps in Chapter III on the brink of sociality. Some of them had nesting behavior with features in common with all social vespids: progressive feeding of the larvae; relatively long-lived mothers staying with their young; and nests containing several young wasps of various ages at one time. Some of these wasps nest communally, with each female of a nesting aggregation caring for her own young. But none of them had a reproductive division of labor of the kind we have just described as being characteristic of the social wasps.

A division of labor does not in itself seem very remarkable to most people, living as we do in societies where job specialization is commonplace and solitary self-sufficiency virtually impossible. Even sterile workers have their counterparts in human societies with old-maid aunts and celibate clergy. But the reproductive division of labor is a biological enigma, for it means that some individuals (e.g., workers) "sacrifice" time and energy caring for the young of others which they could devote to their own offspring. If Darwin was right, these insect spinsters should become quickly extinct, since they leave no offspring to perpetuate their selfless ways.

Darwin worried about this very problem. In *The Origin of Species* he states that at one time he thought the existence of highly modified sterile castes in insects might be "fatal" to his entire theory. However, he resolved the problem by suggesting that natural selection could act on families as well as on individuals, insect societies generally being composed of a mother (or, in termites, a mother and a father) and her own offspring.

During the first half of the twentieth century the social insect family, or colony, was frequently thought of as being a "superorganism" (or "supraorganism") in which the reproductive and nursing functions are carried out by separate castes analogous to the organ systems of an individual organism. This concept also emphasized the unity of the colony as an object of natural selection. The superorganism concept was useful because it helped people to visualize highly integrated insect groups without likening them to human societies. However, like all analogies, the comparison of colonies and organisms is not entirely accurate. An individual organism is a genetic unit in that all of the cells of the body contain replicates of the same set of genes, and it produces gametes containing genes drawn from that set. The superorganism (colony), on the other hand, is not genetically homogeneous, for each female within it has a somewhat different set of genes. Therefore it is somewhat misleading to think of the members of a family as a single evolutionary unit: individuals having even slightly different hereditary makeup may behave differently, and be favored to different degrees by natural selection.

A better understanding of the evolution of social behavior has required a "new twist" to evolutionary theory. Population geneticists, who study heredity in groups of interbreeding organisms, have focused attention on the "gene pool" of a species—the genetic composition of all the individuals of the species taken together. Evolution amounts to a change in the frequency of occurrence of certain genes or genetic combinations in the gene pool; and natural selection is said to favor the individuals whose genotypes are best represented in the gene pool of the following generation of reproducing adults. Starting with this idea, William Hamilton, an English biologist who has recently studied the social wasps of Brazil, elaborated a "genetical theory" of social behavior. He gave quantitative expression to an idea that had been realized but not fully appreciated before: that animals can be expected to help other individuals, even at cost to themselves, providing those individuals are closely enough related to them. This is because relatives have a similar hereditary makeup, so that helping a relative is to a certain extent like helping oneself. Furthermore, the closer the relative the greater should be the selective advantage in giving him aid. It is most profitable for most animals to care for their own offspring, since these are the closest relatives among the younger generation. However, in the Hymenoptera this is not so, for reasons we shall discuss below.

Most animals are "diploid," that is, they inherit two sets of genes, one from the mother and one from the father. However, in the Hymenoptera the female is diploid, but the male is "haploid"—he develops from an unfertilized egg and therefore carries only the maternal set of genes. When the diploid female produces eggs her cells must undergo a "reduction division" so that only one-half her full genetic complement goes into each egg; otherwise a fertilized egg would end up with too many sets of genes. Since each reduction division separated the genes in a different way, each egg contains a somewhat different assortment of the mother's genes. On the other hand, the male cells do not undergo reduction division during gamete production since they each have only one set of genes to begin with. So all of the sperm produced by a single male are genetically identical.

As a result of this mode of reproduction, sisters have an unusually high degree of relationship. Assuming that the mother mated only once, sisters will have identical sets of paternal genes. Thus one-half of their genes—those from their father—will automatically be identical. Of the maternal genes, which make up the remaining halves of their genotypes, not all will be identical. Due to segregation in the diploid mother there is only a half chance that the maternal genes of two daughters are alike. Thus only one-half of the maternal genes are held in common, which is to say that an average of one-fourth of all their genes are identical by descent from the mother. This makes a total of three-fourths of their genes identical.

In most animals this is not the case: in fully diploid species reduction division occurs in both sexes, and mother and father contribute equally to the genotypes of their offspring. Thus sisters have only one-half their genes alike. In both fully diploid and male-haploid (e.g. hymenopteran) species a female has one-half her genes resembling those of a daughter. Thus a young female wasp should theoretically differ from a female of a fully diploid species in preferring to help her mother rear sisters (three-fourths alike) rather than starting her own nest to rear daughters (only one-half alike). This is just what the workers of a wasp colony in fact do.

Societies having large numbers of sterile females have evolved several times in the order Hymenoptera (see Chapter III), and in only one group (the termites) not having the haplo-diploid mode of reproduction. This is evidence that the degree of relationship has indeed been an important factor in the evolution of social life. But one could just as well turn this reasoning about and ask "Why aren't all wasps social?" All of the thousands of solitary wasp species are thought to share the haplo-diploid reproductive system, yet most of them show no trace of sociality. The answer involves the concept of "preadaptation" introduced in Chapter III: for a trait to be a selective advantage the animal must be equipped to use it "in

FIG. 102. Adults and comb of *Vespa saxonica*. The nest envelope has been partially removed; grublike larvae protrude from the cells. (Photograph by László Móczár).

advance" of its occurrence. The preadaptations we discussed in Chapter III were not only a logical series of interactions leading toward sociality as we know it in the vespids and possibly resembling the stages passed through by the ancestors of social wasps. They also suggest the conditions that set the stage for the origin of social behavior—that made it biologically possible for societies to develop among the vespids. Now we can re-examine some of those preadaptations to see how they may have favored the rise of social behavior, for the genetic theory of social behavior brings some new insight into the significance of these preadaptations.

We considered four developments to be preadaptations to sociality: (a) the possession of a nest to which the female returns repeatedly; (b) placement of numerous cells at one site; (c) provisioning more than one cell at a time; and (d) increased longevity of females. All of these would contribute to the likelihood of nesting in groups and, in particular, in groups of close relatives: the establishment of a more or less permanent residence and the ability to return to it provides a potential family gathering place, and the behavioral equipment (place memory and the ability to orient precisely) for gathering there. Placement of numerous cells at one site—clumping rather than dispersal of the brood—is the next step toward keeping the family together. If the female first built a cell cluster, then oviposited there, then provisioned, then sealed all of the cells at one time and left, all of her offspring would be approximately the same age and would have little chance of coexisting in the same place with their mother. So the simple matter of placing an egg in a cell as soon as the cell is completed along with the practice of gradually adding cells to a cluster has great significance: it means that there are offspring of various ages growing up simultaneously in the same nest, with their mother likely to be still provisioning the younger cells while the older offspring approach maturity. In such a situation the mother, whether a mass or a progressive provisioner, might be expected to live increasingly long and eventually to have a lifespan overlapping that of her eldest young. Furthermore, when those first young emerge they would find their mother still attending the cells of their younger siblings. Then they would have the "option" of going off on their own or raising sisters and brothers—that is, becoming "social."

This evolutionary sequence would result in a matrifilial society—a society of mother and daughters—like that of all the social wasps. A conceivable alternative would occur if the daughters nested together even in the absence of a longlived mother. It has been suggested that such a daughter group could develop cooperative brood care and a reproductive division of labor. However, two considerations make it seem somewhat less likely that sociality originated in such sibling groups in the wasps. In such a society the worker sisters would be raising nieces (daughters of a sister rather than their mother) less closely related to them than their own daughters would be; and when such societies occur among wasps (e.g., the foundress associations of *Polistes*) they are only a very shortlived stage in the development of a matrifilial society. However it has been suggested that social behavior could arise in orphaned sibling groups if some of the sisters were markedly enough inferior to others in their ability to reproduce. In that case, they might better help superior sisters than try to compete with them.

This raises an additional important point: degree of relationship is only one of many factors, albeit an important one, that must be considered in explaining the origin and evolution of social life in wasps. As an illustration of this point, even if two females were genetically identical, one would not be expected to cooperate with the other unless the aided female could reproduce more effectively as a result. Conversely, if the aided female would benefit greatly from help (e.g., by greatly increasing her egg production or the number or quality of young reared to maturity) compared to the reproductive ability of the auxiliary on her own, the auxiliary might be expected to sacrifice her personal fertility to help the superior female even if the degree of relationship were quite low. Thus it would be very helpful to a female to be able to judge both her degree of relationship and her relative reproductive capacity in deciding whether to help another or to reproduce independently.

There is evidence that some wasps may have indirect means of making such judgments. In a sense, a female can "estimate" whether or not another individual is a relative by where she is encountered: if she is near the parental nest she is more likely to be a relative than if she is far away from that nest. It has further been suggested that the relative reproductive capacity of an encountered female could be estimated by her position in dominance-subordinance interactions: since more dominant individuals tend to have larger ovaries (in *Polistes*, for example) there is reason to believe that they would be better reproductives. Such a system of "judgments" may actually operate among *Polistes* foundresses, which, as we have seen, form dominance hierarchies in which the dominant female becomes queen and the subordinates become workers. Dominance interactions may thus have promoted the evolution of sociality in wasps by enabling females found in groups to make an advantageous decision about their reproductive role in life—whether to compete as a solitary reproductive or use the superior machinery of a relative by supporting her output. It is also of interest in this connection that cooperating *Polistes* foundresses are usually sisters who have gathered near their parental nest site.

Another factor which may play a role in the evolution of sociality in addition to genetic relationship has been called "predator and parasite pressure." Females might find it advantageous to nest together and cooperate regardless of their degree of relationship if in so doing they more quickly established a nest and guarded it against enemies. If the females of such an association were non-relatives they would be expected to cooperate on an exchange basis, perhaps taking turns at guarding the nest or nursing the brood and foraging, so that the nest would not be left unattended. It is difficult to see how such associations could lead to the evolution of a sterile caste, since a female with any reproductive capacity at all would be more likely to nest on her own than completely devote her life to a non-relative—a practice which would leave her without genetic representation in the next generation. But "predator and parasite pressure" could nonetheless have helped make social life advantageous in the groups of relatives where it most probably originated.

VI. *The Biotic Relationships of Wasps*

No organism can properly be considered apart from its environment, for each species has evolved to fill a particular niche not fully occupied by any other. Only by delineating the relationships of an animal to various environmental factors can we understand its role in nature and the significance of its various structural and behavioral characteristics. In the case of wasps, knowledge of biotic factors, that is, other organisms, is especially important, for wasps depend upon other arthropods and upon plants for food and are attacked by a variety of predators and parasites. Many of their behavior patterns as well as their size, color, and body form represent adaptations for obtaining food with minimum competition with other species and for reducing the incidence of attacks by parasites and predators.

We have mentioned some of these parasites and predators from time to time, but it seems appropriate to take a closer look at them. This will also enable us to discuss certain groups of wasps barely mentioned up to now, groups such as the cuckoo wasps (Chrysididae), velvet ants (Mutillidae) and certain genera and species of Pompilidae, Sphecidae, and Vespidae that have become parasites of other wasps. These can be conveniently grouped as cleptoparasites (i.e., thief-parasites, which develop primarily on the food stored in the cell), social parasites (which usurp colonies of social species), and parasitoids (which consume the wasp larvae). After discussing hymenopterous enemies, we shall take a brief look at various parasitic flies and beetles, the relationships with certain mites, and finally mimetic coloration apparently serving to reduce predation by birds and other vertebrates.

Cleptoparasitic Wasps

The substances stored in the nests of wasps, bees, and ants represent rich supplies of food, and it is perhaps not surprising that a variety of organisms take advantage of this. These are the cleptoparasites (from the Greek *kleptēs*, a thief), sometimes also called brood-parasites or labor-parasites. For the most part they do not feed directly on the cell contents, but deposit an egg so that their larvae may do so. The offspring of the host must, of course, be disposed of, and most cleptoparasites have developed behavioral mechanisms for destroying the egg or larva of the host so that it cannot compete with their own larva for the limited cell contents. Hence cleptoparasites are also predators of a sort, although they attack the host not primarily as food but simply to make its food-store fully available to their own offspring.

It has often been pointed out that many cleptoparasites are closely related to their hosts. For example, the most abundant cleptoparasites of spider wasps are other Pompilidae resembling their hosts very closely. This resemblance extends to even their most subtle structural features and indicates that this is by no means mimicry but a reflection of the fact that parasites and hosts shared a recent common ancestry. In all probability cleptoparasitism began as simple brigandage, that is, as stealing of paralyzed prey as it lay near the nest entrance. This was postulated many years ago by the noted French wasp observer Charles Ferton, who wrote as follows:

"The parasitic habit would . . . appear to have been built up in the following manner: [*Episyron*] *rufipes* [a common pompilid], living in colonies, has acquired the habit of stealing the prey of its neighbor and even of fighting for the possession of prey not its own. Some individuals finally learned to steal the spiders that had been buried, either by driving away the rightful owner while she was sealing the burrow, or by ferreting through the soil occupied by the colony in search of sealed burrows. Their descendents, inheriting this habit, gave up constructing a nest and transporting the stolen prey to it and left it in the cell where it was discovered, simply substituting their egg for the one it bore. Thus [the genus *Evagetes*] was evolved, scarcely distinct from the maternal stock in many of its anatomical characters but become a parasite on the species from which it arose."

This was written in 1905, so perhaps we may forgive Ferton his assumptions that learned behavior may be inherited and that species may evolve in the absence of isolation. Whatever the mechanisms (and the origin of cleptoparasitism and social parasitism is far from fully understood), Ferton may have accurately described some of the intermediate stages. W.M. Wheeler, in an important paper on this subject in 1919, postulated that cleptoparasitism might arise as a result of "urgency of oviposition and temporary or local dearth of the supply of provisions for the offspring."

There are many records of spider wasps taking the paralyzed prey of other individuals, either of the same or different species. In some instances the prey is taken from a plant crotch or other hiding place, in other instances from the burrow entrance or even the burrow itself. Some species seem more inclined to prey-stealing than others, for example the European *Episyron rufipes,* discussed by Ferton, and the North American *Priocnemis cornica.* In Japan, certain individuals of *Batozonellus annulatus* have been seen to dig into nests of other members of the same species, destroy the egg, and substitute their own egg.

Members of the pompilid genus *Evagetes,* as Ferton mentioned, do not hunt spiders but seek out the provisioned nests of spider wasps of other genera, enter them, and substitute their own egg for that of their host. The genus *Evagetes* resembles *Pompilus* so closely that separation of the genera on the basis of museum specimens is sometimes difficult; yet the behavior patterns of the cleptoparasitic genus have undergone a remarkable reorganization. *Evagetes* females spend much of their time walking over the ground in areas where spider wasps are nesting. Their somewhat thickened antennae remain in constant motion over the soil surface, and it is believed that they detect nests by odor or by the "feel" of a filled entrance; often they pause to dig at a certain spot or to explore a depression. If they observe a pompilid nesting, they "freeze" or "hide" behind some object until the pompilid completes its nest and provisions it. Then the *Evagetes* may rush into the nest, even before the host completes the closure; in most recorded instances, the host makes no attempt to drive the parasite away. Once inside the cell, the *Evagetes* removes the host's egg from the spider with its mandibles and chews or even devours it. A moment later it lays its own slightly smaller egg on the spider, then leaves the nest, scraping sand into the burrow behind it. It has been shown that if the spider already happens to bear an *Evagetes* egg, it is nevertheless destroyed and a new one substituted.

The species of *Evagetes* are sometimes very common, so they evidently thrive by taking advantage of the labors of other pompilids. There is another genus of cleptoparasitic pompilids which is less commonly encountered in nature and which is structurally rather different from its hosts, so much so that it is usually placed in a different subfamily. This is the genus *Ceropales*. It is probable that *Ceropales* split off from the stock of spider-hunting pompilids much earlier than *Evagetes;* it has had time to develop many structural differences as well as a more advanced type of cleptoparasitism.

The female *Ceropales* also lurks about where other pompilids are nesting, but her attention is focused not

upon the nest, but upon the spider as it is being trans-
ported to the nest (Fig. 103). At a propitious moment, the
Ceropales leaps upon the spider and quickly inserts her
egg into the book-lungs, where it is invisible or nearly so
from the outside. The tip of the abdomen of *Ceropales* is
compressed and somewhat wedge-shaped, evidently an
adaptation for inserting the egg into the book-lungs. The

FIG. 103. A female *Ceropales maculatus* (left) following close behind a prey-laden female *Pompilus plumbeus* (right). In a moment
the *Ceropales* will quickly attempt to insert her egg into the book-
lungs of the spider, perhaps resulting in a fight between host and
parasite. (Günter Olberg, 1959).

host wasp has often been seen attacking the parasite or attempting to pull the spider away or protect it from the
oviposition thrusts of the *Ceropales*, suggesting that in this
case there has also been time for the evolution of a response of the host to its rather different-appearing parasite. Whether or not the parasite is successful, the pompilid ordinarily completes its nesting and lays an egg on
the spider. If a *Ceropales* egg is also present, it hatches
in a shorter time than the host egg and begins to feed on
the spider first; when the host larva hatches, the *Ceropales*
larva devours it, too. Thus the specializations of *Ceropales*

extend to the hatching time of the egg and the behavior of the larva.

The situation in another major family of solitary wasps, the Sphecidae, parallels that in the Pompilidae very closely. Here also many cases of brigandage have been reported. In highly populous aggregations of *Bembix*, females very commonly pounce upon other females returning with flies and attempt to obtain a firm grasp on the fly and carry it to their own nest—though whether certain females are more likely to do this than others is unknown. Certain *Ammophila* have been reported to exhume caterpillars from the nests of other individuals of the same species. According to the French entomologist L. Chevalier, the small twig-nesting sphecid *Passaloecus corniger* lives primarily as a brigand, the females doing most of their "hunting" in the nests of other wasps that feed upon aphids, especially those of *Psenulus atratus*. However, most species of *Passaloecus* are believed to seek their aphids in vegetation. It is presumably from antecedents similar to these that the two major genera of cleptoparasitic Sphecidae arose: *Stizoides* and *Nysson*.

Stizoides is a genus resembling grasshopper-hunters of the genus *Stizus* very closely, as the name implies. It is assumed that *Stizoides* evolved from a *Stizus*-like ancestor, although all records so far show *Stizoides* attacking grasshopper predators of an unrelated genus, *Prionyx*. It is believed that both olfactory and visual cues are employed by the female *Stizoides* in finding nests of their hosts, and evidently they sometimes enter the nests while the host is still in or near it. *Stizoides* is able to dig into the nest effectively and to close it upon leaving; inside the nest the female apparently destroys the egg of the host and lays her own slightly smaller egg in a different place on the grasshopper. Thus the behavior of these wasps resembles that of *Evagetes* in many ways and probably represents a comparable stage in the evolution of cleptoparasitism.

The situation in the genus *Nysson* is quite different and more comparable to *Ceropales*. *Nysson* is structurally different enough from its hosts to be placed in a different tribe, and as in *Ceropales* the specializations extend to the immature stages, for the egg hatches sooner than that of its host and the young larva seeks out and destroys the egg or larva of the host. In this case the host is *Gorytes* or a related genus of leafhopper or treehopper-hunters, and the parasite lays its egg in a concealed position, such as under the pronotal shield of a treehopper. However, in all observed instances the parasite enters the nest-cell for oviposition rather than laying the egg while the prey is outside, as in *Ceropales;* this would, in fact, be impossible with these wasps, for the prey is carried rapidly and directly to the nest in flight.

The species of *Nysson* are unusual in that they have a rather heavy, deeply pitted integument (to a lesser extent this is also true of *Ceropales*). This is regarded as an adaptation for avoiding the bites and stings of their hosts —a "suit of armor" which can be penetrated only with difficulty. Other wasps which live at the expense of wasps and bees are similarly "armored," for example Sapygidae and Mutillidae. It is in the "cuckoo wasps," the family Chrysididae, that this feature reaches its greatest development. Cuckoo wasps not only have an unusually thick, strongly sculptured integument, but they are capable of rolling into a ball by applying the concave under surface of their abdomen to the under side of the thorax, in this way offering scarcely any target for the attacks of their host (Fig. 104). Cuckoo wasps are also unusual in that they have completely lost the ability to sting. Rather, the whole apical part of the abdomen forms an extensible tube which can be extruded like a telescope at the moment of oviposition into the nest-cell of the host. Cuckoo wasps attack a wide variety of wasps and bees and apparently split off from the main line of wasp evolution a long time ago (perhaps from a bethylidlike ancestor). Most species have bright, metallic colors—green, blue, or coppery red—but so far as we know no one has satisfactorily explained the significance of these unusual colors.

Cuckoo wasps attack ground-nesters, twig-nesters, and the occupants of mud nests, although any one species confines its attacks to one or a few related species occurring

FIG. 104. A cuckoo wasp (*Chrysis parvula*) in the rolled-up position assumed when attacked. The shieldlike abdomen is concave beneath, and protects the vulnerable parts of the head and thorax. (U.S. Department of Agriculture).

in similar habitats. The female *Chrysis coerulans*, for example, flies about in areas where various twig-nesting Eumenidae are active; when a eumenid is observed provisioning a nest, she remains in the area, facing the nest with rapidly vibrating antennae. When the host wasp stops bringing in caterpillars and starts to bring mud with which to seal the cell, the cuckoo wasp responds by quickly backing into the hole while the host is absent and, by extruding her telescoped apical abdominal segments, lays an egg among the prey in the cell. She then leaves the nest but may continue to lurk about and eventually lay her eggs in several cells in the series. The egg of the cuckoo wasp hatches either before or after that of the host. The newly hatched larva has a large head with long antennae and sharp, piercing mandibles, and the body may have long setae or pseudopods that assist it in moving about in the cell. Having found the egg or small larva of the host and destroyed it, the cuckoo wasp larva molts to a more grublike form and proceeds to consume the provisions in the cell, eventually spinning its cocoon there. It is interesting that when *Chrysis coerulans* parasitizes several cells in one nest she generally lays female-producing eggs in the innermost cells, male-producing eggs in the outermost, like her eumenid host; also, the larvae orientate themselves toward the open end of the boring by means of the convexity or concavity of the cell walls, as do their hosts.

Chrysis coerulans attacks twig-nesting eumenids of several genera, all of which utilize caterpillars or beetle larvae as prey. *Omalus aeneus* also attacks members of several genera of twig-nesters, but in this case all aphid-hunting Sphecidae. *Chrysogona verticalis* evidently restricts its attacks to spider-hunters of the genus *Trypoxylon,* while *Neochrysis panamensis* attacks cockroach-hunters of the genus *Podium.* Thus while certain species attack more than one host species (or even genus), they do appear to confine themselves to one type of host prey.

Some of the cuckoo wasps which attack mud-nesters are reported to break into closed cells for oviposition, and some of the parasites of ground-nesters dig through closed nest entrances. These species have not been well studied, but there is good reason to believe that at least some of them are not cleptoparasites but parasitoids, developing at the expense of the host larva rather than the provisions in the cell. We shall therefore defer discussion of these Chrysididae for a later section of this chapter.

In summary, it may be said that cleptoparasitism, or the "cuckoo habit," has arisen many times independently among wasps: at least twice in the Pompilidae (*Evagetes* and *Ceropales*), at least twice in the Sphecidae (*Stizoides* and the Nyssonini), and also in the large family Chrysididae. The wasp family Sapygidae must also be included here, although the species that have been studied are cleptoparasites of bees, not wasps. There are also many genera of bees which have become cleptoparasites of other bees. Social parasitism, as found in the Vespidae, and also among bumblebees as well as many ants, is a closely related phenomenon which we shall explore shortly. In sum, cleptoparasitism and social parasitism have appeared among the higher Hymenoptera literally dozens of times, each time conferring upon their practitioners major modifications in behavior and structure—including such things as loss of hunting behavior, unusual modes of nest entry and oviposition, a thickened body integument, modifications in sense organs, and (in social species) loss of a worker caste. All of this is especially interesting because of the parallelisms among birds. Not only the cuckoos, but also the cowbirds and members of at least three other families of birds have developed mechanisms for insuring that their offspring be reared through the labors of other species of birds.

Social Parasites

The terms cleptoparasitism and social parasitism are sometimes used interchangeably, but we prefer to restrict the latter to parasites of social species which use their hosts as a work force rather than as a direct source of food. The female social parasite waits until the queen of a colony has established her nest and reared a number of worker offspring. Then she enters the nest and usurps the position of the rightful queen, preventing her further reproduction by either killing her, driving her away, or eating her eggs. The host workers tolerate the foreign queen and care for her young as they would the offspring of their own mother. The result is that the colony eventually comes to consist mostly if not entirely of adults of the parasite species—all males and females, as no workers are produced.

Among the vespid wasps at least seven species are known to be obligatory social parasites; that is, the females are incapable of founding their own colonies independently and produce no workers of their own. So closely do the parasites resemble their hosts that most of them have been recognized only within the last thirty years. All are associated with the best-studied genera of social wasps (*Vespula* and *Polistes*), suggesting that investigation of the many tropical social wasps whose biology is almost unknown will reveal others. European workers have tended to put the parasitic *Polistes* in a separate genus (*Sulcopolistes*) and the parasitic *Vespula* in two separate genera (*Pseudovespula* and *Vespula,* restricting the names *Paravespula* and *Dolichovespula* to the nonparasitic species). This nomenclature is not only unduly complicated but tends to conceal the fact that the relationship of parasite and host is very close indeed, and in each case the parasite may well have evolved from a common ancestor with its host. Parasites differ from their hosts in having a more heavily sclerotized integument, larger head and mandibles, and in some cases a stronger, recurved sting—all adaptations probably useful in fighting.

In *Polistes* the interactions of hosts and parasites have been observed directly by Joachim Sheven in Europe. He found that the parasites act as superdominant individuals, overcoming the original inhabitants one by one with an exaggerated form of the dominance behavior common in *Polistes* colonies (see Chapter IV). The female of *Polistes* ("*Sulcopolistes*") *atrimandibularis* touches the host (*P. bimaculatus* or *P. omissus*) "slowly and intensively with the antennae, slowly riding upon her, and at last . . . bending the abdomen and aiming the sting against the waist and neck of the dominated animal." However, the usurper usually does not kill the host queen, which remains on the nest until she disappears or dies of other causes. *P. se-menowi* (parasite of *P. gallicus* and *P. nimpha*) and *P. sulcifer* (parasite of *P. gallicus*) use less violent methods, with less stinging and more antennal striking.

The takeover of a *Vespula* colony by a social parasite has apparently never been observed, but a partial reconstruction of events is possible from inspection of the contents of parasitized nests. Sometimes the body of the host queen is found, indicating that she was killed by the usurper; and in one nest of the European *Vespula sylvestris*, parasitized by a female of *V. omissa*, eight host workers were found dead near the corpse of their deposed queen, apparently having come to her aid in vain. In North America, it is not uncommon to find colonies of the common yellow jacket *Vespula arenaria* which have been parasitized by a species having white markings instead of yellow, *Vespula arctica*. In the early summer, parasitized nests are not likely to be recognized, since they contain many *arenaria* workers plus one female *arctica* and some of her brood, but by August the *arenaria* workers dwindle in numbers and a colony of yellow-jackets becomes transformed into a colony of "white jackets," all of whom are queens and males.

There are two known "facultative" social parasites (i.e., parasites capable of living and thriving under more than one set of conditions) whose habits shed some light on the mode of evolution of obligatory social parasitism. These species, *Vespula squamosa* and *Vespa dybowskii*, are capable of founding colonies independently and always produce some workers of their own. But sometimes they take over colonies established by queens of other species (respectively: *Vespula vidua;* and *Vespa crabro* or *V. xanthoptera*). Both species nest somewhat later than those they parasitize; and one observer noted a similarity between the nesting sites of host and parasite. Thus the original social parasites may in some cases have been aggressive, late-nesting females who encountered established nests while searching for nesting sites of their own.

Parasitoid Wasps

In this section we shall consider certain wasps that develop as parasitoids of other wasps, that is, their larvae feed not on the food provided them but directly on the larva of the host, generally after it has completed its feeding. Two major groups fall in this category: (1) certain kinds of true (aculeate) wasps (Mutillidae, some Chrysididae), which have become parasitoids secondarily and (2) some of the true parasitoids (Terebrantia: a few ichneumon, chalcid, and trigonalid wasps) which have taken to attacking wasp larvae in their nest-cells rather than free-living or boring larvae of other orders. Members of the first group attack only solitary wasps, but members of the second group attack both solitary and social species.

It is probable that the majority of Chrysididae are cleptoparasites, as the name "cuckoo wasps" implies. Their larvae do, of course, destroy the egg or larva of their host, in the manner of many cleptoparasites, and in at least one case it has been shown that the chrysidid larva fails to feed upon the cell contents and to grow if it is deprived of its initial meal, the host larva. From such an antecedent has apparently developed the delayed development of some of the more specialized chrysidids, such as members of the genus *Parnopes*. The female *Parnopes edwardsii* enters the nest of ground-nesting fly-predators of genera such as *Bembix* and *Steniolia,* often while the host wasps are actively provisioning. *Steniolia* females have been seen to attack the parasite vigorously, attempting to sting it and even carrying the coiled-up *Parnopes* several inches and dropping it. When the cuckoo wasp is successful in entering a cell containing a partially grown larva (*Steniolia* and *Bembix* are progressive provisioners), she lays her egg on the larva and departs. The egg hatches in a few days, but the *Parnopes* larva feeds very little at first and remains as a very small grub attached to the thorax of the host larva until the latter spins its cocoon. Then the chrysidid larva begins to feed more actively, and within a week or ten days it consumes the host larva and spins its own cocoon inside that of the host. Thus by some physiological mechanism permitting a delay in growth until after the host has completed feeding, these chrysidids have been converted from cleptoparasites to parasitoids of an unusual kind.

One of the chrysidid parasites of mud-daubers (*Sceliphron*) evidently lays its egg after the cell has already been closed and the host larva has spun its cocoon. In this case the female cuckoo wasp, *Chrysis fuscipennis*, makes a conical hole through the wall of the mud cell and lays its egg through the breach; upon withdrawal of the ovipositor the hole is sealed with a brown plug probably formed from a secretion of the wasp. The *Chrysis* larva then consumes the pupa of the *Sceliphron* and spins its own cocoon, later emerging by chewing a hole through the mud closing plug. It seems odd that this apparently specialized mode of entry and parasitism occurs in the same genus as other cleptoparasitic species such as *Chrysis coerulans*, discussed on an earlier page. In the vast majority of chrysidids, we do not know the manner of entry into the host cell or whether development is primarily upon the prey or upon the host larva.

Mutillidae ("velvet ants") apparently always attack larvae after they·have spun their cocoons. The females enter nests already containing cocoons, either by digging through the soil or breaking through the walls of mud nests or the closing plugs of nests in twigs. They then chew a hole through the wall of the cocoon, turn around and insert an egg through the hole and onto the diapausing host larva, and finally seal up the hole in the cocoon with salivary fluids and particles of soil or mud.

Mutillids do not appear to be highly host-specific; some species attack wasps of several species or genera or even of more than one family, and at least one species appears to attack certain bees as well as wasps. Others attack various ground-nesting or twig-nesting bees, and a few even attack the puparia of flies such as the tsetse fly, sealing up the hole in the puparium in much the way that the hole in the cocoon is sealed. Certain Mutillidae are reported to attack adult bees or wasps, including honey-bees and *Bembix*, biting the host in the neck region and sucking out its body contents.

Unlike cuckoo wasps, Mutillidae possess a powerful sting. Since the sting is not needed for subduing the host, which is normally quiescent inside its cocoon, it is usually assumed that it serves in defense against the attacks of the host or against vertebrate predators. Female Mutillidae are wingless and often spend long hours walking over the soil in a conspicuous manner, so it is possible that the sting serves them well in escaping the attacks of birds, lizards, and other vertebrates. Female Mutillidae display some of the most vivid and unusual color patterns of any insects, often including orange or red bands or spots, and it is probably safe to conclude that these are "warning colors." That is, an animal that discovers that the mutillid is hard-bodied and a powerful stinger is likely to remember its brilliant and unusual color pattern and to avoid it in the future. The violent stings of mutillids have earned them such names as "cow-killers" and "mule-killers" (Fig. 105).

In contrast to cuckoo wasps and mutillids, the ichneumon wasps which attack Aculeata have little capacity for digging or for forcing entry through mud barriers. Consequently they do not attack ground-nesting species, and their mode of attacking twig-nesters or mud-daubers is to pierce the twig or the cell with their long ovipositor and to lay one or more eggs on the host larva or pupa. Some of these ichneumons (e.g., *Ephialtes spatulata*, an enemy of certain twig-nesting Eumenidae) are related to species which attack wood-boring beetle larvae, and they lay their eggs in the cells of twig-nester by simply drilling through the wood. Members of the ichneumon genera *Messatoporus* and *Acroricnus* attack the occupants of mud nests, apparently by drilling through the walls of the cells. Members of a related genus, *Pachysomoides,* are among the most interesting of these parasites, for they

FIG. 105. A female mutillid wasp, also called "velvet ant" or "cow-killer." (U.S. Department of Agriculture).

restrict their attacks to nests of social paper wasps of the genus *Polistes* (see Chapter IV; Fig. 84). As many as eight parasitoid larvae may develop on a single *Polistes* larva or pupa, eventually spinning their small cocoons in the base of the *Polistes* cell. Nests may be attacked early or late in the season, and occasionally as many as 35 percent of the *Polistes* larvae may be parasitized.

Even populous colonies of hornets and yellow jackets (Vespinae) are not immune to the attacks of ichneumon wasps. The parasite in this case is *Sphecophaga burra,* and it is reported to attack aerial nests of the bald-faced hornet as well as aerial and terrestrial nests of various species of yellow jackets, although little is known of the mode of entry and oviposition. A related, European species is said to oviposit on the wasp larva, but the parasite does not develop until the host has spun its cocoon and pupated. Up to seven parasites may develop on a single host larva. After devouring the wasp pupa, the parasites spin their cocoons in the bottom of the cell.

Several species of chalcid wasps are also known to be wasp parasites. Since these are minute insects, many individuals may develop within a single wasp larva. The best known of these chalcids is *Melittobia chalybii,* a wasp little more than 1 millimeter long, over 500 of which may develop at the expense of a single wasp larva. This parasite has been reared from a wide variety of mud-daubers

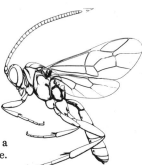

FIG. 106. *Sphecophaga vesparum,* a parasite of social Vespinae in Europe. (H.K. Townes, 1962).

as well as twig-nesting wasps and bees. In the laboratory it will attack the larvae of social wasps as well as ground-nesting solitary wasps, but those are probably not often attacked in the field. (In fact, in the laboratory *Melittobia* attacks and develops successfully on insects as diverse as cockroaches and beetles, and it is often a serious laboratory pest.)

The males of *Melittobia chalybii* are short-lived and are greatly outnumbered by the females; they have short, nonfunctional wings and generally fertilize the females as soon as they molt to the adult stage. The males are reported to be "belligerent" and to "engage in mortal combat with one another." According to one author, even a dead male, or a part of one, "will be fiercely pounced upon by another male, and dragged around and thrown about with a great show of anger, like a terrier with a rat." Fertilized females leave the cell by boring through the cap. They evidently seek out fresh wasp nest-cells by walking and hopping; although their wings are fully developed, they seem to fly little if at all.

Having found a suitable host, the female remains with it for the remainder of her life of two or three months. She pierces the integument frequently and feeds at the exuding blood; after a few days, when her eggs have matured, she begins to lay several eggs a day on the host. Her first few (twelve to twenty) offspring develop rapidly and produce another generation of adults within two to three weeks. These adults differ in several respects from their parents: the males are blind and have even shorter wings, and the females have crumpled wings and stout abdomens (Fig. 107). These females are able to lay eggs immediately and at a more rapid pace than their mother, but they live only a few days. The eggs laid by these females—and the remainder of the offspring of the mother—undergo a slow development, and after about 90 days (or after a winter diapause) give rise to offspring of the "normal" type. R.G. Schmieder, who was the first to

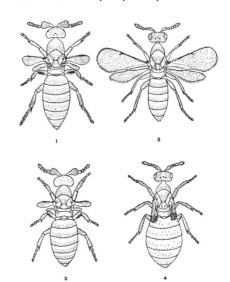

FIG. 107. *Melittobia chalybii,* a ubiquitous chalcid parasite of many kinds of wasp larvae. 1 and 3 are males, 2 and 4 females. The upper two figures (1 and 2) are of the "normal" form, the lower two (3 and 4) of the rapid-developing form in which the males are blind, the females robust and short-winged. (R.G. Schmieder, 1933).

elucidate this unusual life cycle, believed that the larvae of these rapid-developing, short-lived individuals fed on the blood of the host, while the others fed on less nutritious tissues (experimentally, the eggs of either form were equally capable of producing offspring of either form). This instance of dimorphism resulting from the nature of the larval food is in some ways suggestive of caste determination in social insects. In this case, the two forms together serve to build up a population of several hundred offspring able to utilize fully the larva of the host wasp.

Before leaving the hymenopterous enemies of wasps, we should mention briefly a group having perhaps the most remarkable life cycles of all: the Trigonalidae. These wasps bear some resemblance to ichneumons, but their ovipositor is reduced and their wing venation more like that of true wasps; in fact, the group is an isolated one of uncertain position in the classification of Hymenoptera. The adult females lay great numbers of small eggs on leaves, where they remain unhatched unless and until the leaf is eaten by a caterpillar (experimentally, they can be induced to hatch by abrading them in weak caustic pot-ash). The eggs normally hatch in the digestive tract of the caterpillar and bore their way into the body cavity, but here they fail to develop to maturity unless the cater-pillar itself is ingested—either by an ichneumon parasite living internally or if the caterpillar is collected by a wasp and carried to the nest as food for its larva. One species, *Lycogaster pullata,* is able to develop either on ichneu-mon parasites of caterpillars or in the nests of eumenid wasps that collect caterpillars, in each case as a parasitoid of the hymenopterous larva or pupa. Another North Amer-ican species, *Bareogonalos canadensis,* has been reared from the nests of *Vespula* in the western states, and a Japanese species has been found to parasitize two spe-cies of *Vespa.* In these cases the small trigonalid larvae are assumed to reach the vespid larva by way of the bolus of macerated food presented by the workers. Considering the remote route by which trigonalids find their true hosts, it is perhaps not surprising that even though the females may lay more than a thousand eggs in one day, these are regarded as very rare insects.

Predatory, Parasitoid, and Cleptoparasitic Flies

Many true flies (Diptera) attack wasps, and some of these are among their most abundant and ubiquitous enemies. Several different, unrelated groups of flies are involved, and their modes of attack are diverse, their life histories sometimes as unusual as some of the parasitoid wasps. Whereas none of the latter attack adult wasps, two kinds of flies do attack adults, one as direct predators (the Asilidae, or assassin flies), the other as parasitoids (the Conopidae). Members of both families are sometimes remarkably wasplike in appearance; they often have banded color patterns like wasps, as well as a slender body form, and some conopids even have a constriction or "wasp waist" toward the center of their body. These

FIG. 108. An assassin fly (Asilidae). (U.S. Department of Agriculture).

have sometimes been cited as examples of "aggressive mimicry," that is, they are said to resemble their hosts so as to be able to approach them closely prior to their attacks. However, most of them bear no close resemblance to the species they attack, and in fact most Asilidae are rather unselective predators on Hymenoptera. Thus it seems more likely that this is simple Batesian mimicry: that is, since these flies inhabit situations containing large numbers of Hymenoptera, it is to their advantage to "look like wasps" so that they will be so treated by birds and other vertebrate predators.

Certain Asilidae bear a striking resemblance to *Polistes* wasps, but studies have shown that some of them do not often attack *Polistes;* rather, they prey upon a wide variety of wasps and bees, principally upon fossorial species that are common in the open, bare areas which the asilids inhabit. Some assassin flies are strikingly similar to bumblebees, but analysis of their prey reveals that they, too, prey upon a variety of bees and wasps. On occasion, certain asilids capture social wasps in considerable numbers, and the larger species sometimes take wasps as large as some of the tarantula hawks (*Pepsis*). Asilids often perch on vegetation overlooking the nesting or flower-visitation sites of wasps and bees. From time to time they fly off swiftly and grapple with flying insects of appropriate size and appearance, when successful holding them in their long, spiny legs and sucking out their blood through a stout beak, which is usually inserted through the membrane of the neck region. The limp and empty bodies of the prey are then discarded.

Conopid flies are less commonly encountered in nature than asilids, but they are more host-specific and their relationship with their hosts is more intimate. One of the best-studied species is *Physocephala texana,* which occurs over most of North America and attacks several species of *Bembix.* The female *Physocephala* perches upon vegetation overlooking nesting sites of *Bembix* and from time to time flies after an adult *Bembix* of either sex (Fig. 109). If successful in overtaking a wasp, the fly alights on its back (usually forcing it to the ground), then inserts an egg beneath one of the abdominal tergites by means of a specialized, horny ovipositor. The larva develops inside the abdomen of the adult wasp, eventually forming its puparium there after causing the death of the wasp. Although *Physocephala* flies are sometimes locally abundant, they probably cause no major reduction in wasp populations. Male wasps are more commonly attacked than females, since they spend more time outside the nest, and

FIG. 109. A conopid fly. This is *Physocephala texana,* perched on a flower overlooking an aggregation of nesting *Bembix* sand wasps.

females which are attacked are able to continue nesting for at least a few days before succumbing.

Other species of Conopidae attack wasps of other genera, but few of these have been well studied. The European *Conops scutellatus* is said to congregate in some numbers around the nests of social Vespidae and to pounce upon the workers as they enter. In some cases, conopids have been seen entering the nests of certain wasps and bees, but whether they attack the adults inside the nests is unknown.

The most ubiquitous parasitoids of wasp larvae are flies of the family Bombyliidae, often called bee-flies because their stout, hairy bodies give them a somewhat bee-like appearance. The adults are often observed feeding at the nectar of flowers, and the females also spend much time in the habitats of the solitary wasps and bees which serve as their hosts (other bee-flies attack the egg masses of grasshoppers or the larvae of beetles and other insects). The females lay great numbers of eggs, not on the host but in or near its nest, and the newly hatched bombyliid larva must seek out the larva or cocoon of its host. The larva is admirably suited for this, since it has an elongate body bearing a number of ambulatory bristles and is somewhat resistant to desiccation (Fig. 110). Species which attack larvae in their cocoons (for example, the species figured, which attacks *Tiphia*) begin to feed im-

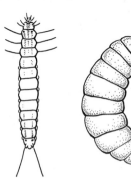

FIG. 110. The larvae of a bee-fly, *Hyperalonia oenamaus*, a parasite of the larvae of *Tiphia* wasps. On the left is a first-stage larva, greatly enlarged, on the right a third-stage larva shown with less enlargement. (After C.P. Clausen, 1928).

mediately and soon transform to a more grublike form. But individuals entering nests containing larvae only partially grown wait until the latter mature and pupate before consuming them and pupating within their cocoons.

Species that attack *Tiphia* and other wasps that do not build a nest evidently scatter their eggs on the soil in places likely to harbor the white grubs of the host. Those which attack wasps or bees in their nesting burrows characteristically hover in front of open burrows and flick their eggs into the entrances. They will, however, oviposit in almost any open hole—such as holes made with a pencil, or even the eyelets of shows. It is often possible to collect the eggs and small larvae of these flies by sinking small, open vials into the sand, for these are readily accepted as oviposition sites. Obviously a very high percentage of the newly hatched larvae must fail to find a host. This is compensated for by the very large numbers of eggs laid by the females; some are capable of laying several thousand eggs in the course of their lives, and gravid females may carry as many as five hundred mature eggs at one time.

As might be suspected, most bee-flies are not highly host-specific, but the small larvae will accept almost any wasp or bee larva which they encounter in the habitat. *Exoprosopa fascipennis* (Fig. 111), for example, attacks a number of ground-nesting Sphecidae as well as *Tiphia* (Tiphiidae). *Anthrax aterrimus* attacks twig-nesting wasps, and accepts a variety of Sphecidae and Eumenidae, while *Anthrax limulatus* hovers in front of open cells in mud nests, flipping its eggs into the entrance, the larvae developing either on the mud-dauber larva or that of various wasps or bees which reuse old mud nests. K.V. Krombein has found that *Lepidophora lepidocera,* an odd-looking bee-fly occurring in Florida, has a larva that commences to feed immediately on the cell contents of certain twig-nesters; furthermore, having consumed the contents of one cell, it breaks through to another cell and consumes

FIG. 111. An adult bee-fly, *Exoprosopa fascipennis*, parasite of various ground-nesting wasps.

its contents also. Thus this species cannot be classified as a parasitoid but must be considered a particularly voracious kind of cleptoparasite.

Cleptoparasitism is also the mode of life of many flies bearing a general resemblance to small house flies which are among the most abundant parasites of solitary wasps. These flies are classified with the flesh-flies (Sarcophagidae), where they make up a special subfamily, the Miltogramminae. There are several genera, each of which has its own particular method of attack. In all genera, the eggs apparently hatch just as they are laid, so that one or more small maggots appear on the prey or in the cell. So far as known, miltogrammine maggots develop primarily on the prey in the cell, although the egg or small larva of the host is usually attacked and destroyed promptly. The cell contents are reduced to a putrid mass within a few days, and if the maggots are still not fully fed they may move to an adjacent cell (in the case of aerial nests or of closely grouped cells of nests in the ground). The puparia are formed in the soil near the cell or, in the case of mud nests or nests in twigs, in the cell itself. Many Miltogramminae go through several generations a year even in the northern United States, successive generations often attacking quite different hosts. Most species of this group are not at all host-specific, attacking solitary wasps of many genera and even of several families indiscriminately.

However, certain genera (*Amobia,* for example) attack only aerial nesters, while other genera (such as *Senotainia, Metopia,* and *Phrosinella*) restrict their attacks to ground-nesters.

Members of the genus *Senotainia* have been called "satellite flies," since they follow close behind wasps laden with prey, awaiting an opportunity to slip in quickly and larviposit on the prey, an opportunity often presented as the wasp pauses upon entering the nest (Fig. 113). The flies evidently respond to the image of the prey-laden wasp, but not to that of the nest entrance; now and then flies may be seen following wasps not carrying prey, or even parasites such as Mutillidae, but they quickly move to prey-laden wasps when these are detected, flying a few centimeters behind and usually somewhat below them. The species of *Amobia* also locate the aerial nests of their hosts by following the wasps, but in this case the flies slip into the cells and deposit larvae among the prey.

FIG. 112. A satellite fly, *Senotainia trilineata,* that has landed on a nail being used as an artificial nest-maker. These flies typically follow prey-laden wasps to their nests, then perch nearby after the wasps have entered.

FIG. 113. A digger wasp, *Philanthus zebratus*, scraping open her nest while carrying a bee with her middle legs. Directly behind her is a satellite fly, *Senotainia trilineata*, about to larviposit on the prey.

In both *Amobia* and *Senotainia*, areas of the compound eyes have enlarged facets, presumably an adaptation for "shadowing" the wasps.

In contrast, members of the genus *Metopia* are "hole searchers," seeking out open holes in the ground, entering them, and larvipositing on the prey in the cell. *Phrosinella* also enters nests for larviposition, but in this case the flies appear to be attracted to closed nest entrances; the flies have enlarged front tarsi and are effective diggers (Fig. 114). Thus it appears that ground-nesting wasps are subject to attack whatever their nesting behavior: if the entrance is closed, *Phrosinella* (or mutillids) may enter, and *Senotainia* may larviposit during the pause at the entrance for removing the closure; but if the entrance is left open, *Metopia* may enter, or bee-flies may oviposit into the hole. Presumably the various kinds of closure, mound-leveling, accessory burrows, and so forth, evolved in response to these parasites, certain ones of which probably predominated in certain areas and at certain times in the past, when the behavior patterns evolved. Progressive provisioning may have evolved primarily as a mechanism for avoiding the attacks of parasites, for the continued presence of the mother in the nest (and the evolution of cell-cleaning behavior in some species) must surely reduce the success of these natural enemies. Also, a progressive provisioner makes a portion of its provisioning trips to nests containing relatively developed larvae, and thus stands less chance of introducing *Senotainia* maggots into a nest containing an egg or small larva. If such maggots are introduced later they do not necessarily result in the death of the wasp larva, as the mother is able to increase the amount of prey brought in. The existing evidence suggests that in fact progressive provisioners such as *Bembix* suffer little mortality from miltogrammine flies.

In addition to the flies we have mentioned, several other kinds have been found breeding occasionally in the cells of wasps, chiefly on detritus. The most prevalent of these

FIG. 114. *Phrosinella pilosifrons,* a miltogrammine fly that is capable of entering concealed nests of digger wasps by digging through the closure.

scavengers are members of the genera *Megaselia* and *Dohrniphora* (family Phoridae). These flies are not restricted to wasps' nests, but attack various dead insects occurring in specific habitats. However, they sometimes cause mortality to wasp larvae by rendering the prey unsuitable as food; there is also evidence that maggots of *Megaselia aletiae*, at least, may attack the immature stages of twig-nesting wasps directly.

In summary, it is evident that flies of several groups are major enemies of wasps. On the balance sheet, however, it should not be forgotten that a great many wasps utilize flies as prey. Curiously, it has often been noted that wasps almost never utilize as prey the flies which attack them, even though these flies are often prevalent around the nests. For example, Conopidae are very rarely used as prey; wasps that prey extensively on Bombyliidae rarely take *Exoprosopa* or other wasp parasites; and Miltogramminae seem to be used as prey very rarely, even though related flies of similar size are often used in great numbers. Presumably these flies have evolved behavioral traits which somehow permit them to remain outside the range of the wasps' predatory patterns.

Beetles as Enemies of Wasps

Beetles (Coleoptera) make up the largest order of insects, and occur in virtually every habitat occupied by wasps. Ground beetles and their larvae (Carabidae) are predators of minor importance in the nests of ground-dwellers, and tiger beetles (Cicindelidae) have been observed "stealing" the prey of wasps. Checkered beetles (Cleridae) are often prevalent in burrows in wood and are predatory as adults and as larvae; at least one species is known to feed upon wasp larvae in their cells. However, by far the most interesting coleopterous enemies belong to two families of parasitic beetles having no common name and only rarely encountered as adults in nature: the Rhipiphoridae and the Stylopidae.

Adult Rhipiphoridae are short-lived and of peculiar appearance: in most species the elytra (wing-covers) are short, and the antennae rather bushy. In some cases, at least, the eggs are laid in great numbers in flowers likely to be visited by the hosts, and when they hatch the rather long-legged, hard-bodied larvae are able to wait at least several days for an opportunity to attach themselves to a wasp and be carried to the nest. In the nest, the minute

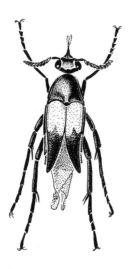

FIG. 115. *Macrosiagon flavipenne*, a rhipiphorid beetle that is a parasite of *Bembix* wasps.

beetle larva drops off the wasp and develops as a parasitoid of the wasp larva. At first it feeds internally, then emerges and feeds externally, the full-grown beetle larva differing greatly in appearance from the newly hatched larva. *Macrosiagon flabellatum* occurs in Europe and attacks eumenids of the genus *Euodynerus;* in North America *Macrosiagon cruentum* also attacks eumenids in twig and mud nests, while *Macrosiagon flavipenne* is a parasite of ground-nesting Sphecidae of the genus *Bembix* (Fig. 115). Still other members of this genus attack Tiphiidae and Scoliidae. In only a very few cases have the life histories of these beetles been worked out in detail.

A European rhipiphorid, *Metoecus paradoxus,* is reported to be a parasitoid of social Vespinae (*Vespula*). In this instance the eggs are laid in crevices in decaying wood in the autumn, where they remain dormant until spring. The newly hatched larvae are presumably carried to the nests by female wasps gathering pulp for nest construction. Once in the nest, the larvae spend their first stage as internal parasites of the wasp larvae, then emerge and encircle the anterior part of the host like a collar, finally pupating in the cell of the wasp. This interesting beetle has not been reported from North America.

FIG. 116. A male stylopid beetle. These curious insects are rarely seen except by persons who collect stylopized wasps (Fig. 117) or other insects and rear them from them.

Members of the family Stylopidae are even more unusual in appearance and in their life cycles, so much so that they have sometimes been placed not among the beetles but in a separate order of insects, called the Strepsiptera or twisted-winged insects. The adult males are minute insects with large eyes, branched antennae, very short elytra, and large, fan-shaped wings (Fig. 116). The females, in contrast, have no wings or elytra and usually no eyes or legs. In most cases the females never emerge fully from their hosts, but remain inside a saclike puparium (hardened last larval skin) which protrudes from between the abdominal segments of the adult host (Fig. 117). An insect bearing one or more of these puparia is said to be "stylopized." Certain genera of Stylopidae attack grasshoppers, others attack leafhoppers, stinkbugs, ants, bees, or wasps. Members of the genus *Xenos* attack *Polistes* and related social wasps, while members of the genus *Pseu-*

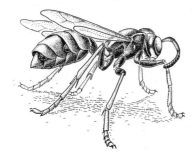

FIG. 117. A "stylopized" *Polistes* wasp. The protruding objects are called "puparia," although they may represent either puparia of males or adult, larviform females.

doxenos attack solitary wasps, including ground-nesters such as *Ammophila* as well as twig-nesting Sphecidae and Eumenidae.

Male Stylopidae emerge from their puparia and fly about very actively, but they live for only a few hours, during which time they attempt to locate a female and to copulate with her. They do this by climbing upon her while vibrating their wings rapidly and inserting a large, hook-shaped aedeagus or intromittent organ, into her puparium. Since the female protrudes from the host with her anterior end out, the sperm are introduced anteriorly and must swim actively through a "brood canal" between the wall of the puparium and the body of the female; the female has no true genital opening, and sperm enter her body cavity through special ducts closed with epithelium. After fertilization, the eggs develop directly into active, long-legged larvae not unlike those of rhipiphorids, and these eventually leave the female via the brood canal, several hundred or even thousands of them emerging from a single female within a short time. Emergence from the host often occurs on flowers, and the larvae are able to live without food for several days until they are able to attach themselves to a wasp and be carried to the nest. It is possible that stylopid larvae sometimes emerge while the host is in the nest, but probably not often, as stylopized females usually participate in few if any nest-building activities.

Once in the wasp nest, the stylopid larvae penetrate the egg or larva of the wasp. Here they develop slowly among the tissues of the growing wasp larva, molting several times and finally forming their puparia at about the time the wasp pupates. Extrusion of the puparium from between the abdominal segments occurs during the pupal stage of the host or within the first few days of adult life. Several stylopids may develop in a single host without causing its death; in fact, stylopized wasps may live as long as unstylopized ones. Although stylopized females usually do not hunt prey or build nests, the males apparently do often mate successfully. Stylopized social wasps, such as *Polistes*, differ little from normal wasps except for the protrusions from between the abdominal segments, but stylopized solitary wasps and bees often show various structural abnormalities. These abnormalities often consist of the presence of female features in male wasps and of male features in females. Such 'intersexes" are evidently the result of nutritional imbalance influencing developmental processes. Social wasps evidently receive more food as they develop and thus appear more normal. It is known that stylopized *Polistes* larvae feed for a longer time than usual, apparently to compensate for the food loss to the parasites. Incidentally, it is perfectly correct to

FIG. 118. A dead and distorted egg of the eumenid wasp *Euodynerus foraminatus apopkensis* containing five firstinstar larvae of the stylopid beetle *Pseudoxenos hookeri*. In this instance multiple penetration of the egg by these larvae has evidently caused the death of the embryo. (Krombein, 1967).

call stylopids "parasites," for, like true parasites, they do not kill their hosts.

Relationships of Mites and Wasps

Mites (Acarina) are minute arthropods related to spiders and having eight legs as adults. They are exceedingly abundant in nature and diverse in their life cycles and feeding behavior. It is not surprising that mites are sometimes found on adult wasps or in their nests, but it does often come as a surprise to learn that some mites have developed so intimate a relationship with certain wasps that they cannot exist apart from their host and that some wasps have evolved specialized integumental grooves or pouches (called acarinaria) for housing their mite symbionts.

Before examining the more specialized mite-wasp relationships, we should take a brief look at some of the less intimate associations. The so-called grain itch mite, *Pyemotes ventricosus,* occurs very widely in nature and feeds on a wide variety of insects. When these mites gain access to a wasp nest, they may consume either the wasp egg, larva, or pupa, or the prey in the cell. Laboratory cultures of these or other insects sometimes become seriously infested with itch mites.

Other species of mites infest wasp nests chiefly as scavengers, and some of these are more or less host-specific. For example, *Vidia concellaria* is an intimate associate of the ground-nesting beetle-predator *Cerceris arenaria* in Europe. The adult and immature mites live in the cells of the wasp, feeding upon remains of beetles not fed upon by the wasp larva. When the latter spins its cocoon, the immature mites remain in the debris attached to the cocoon, and when the adult wasp emerges in the spring the mites attach themselves to its body. As soon as the female makes and provisions a cell, the mites drop off, then grow to maturity and lay their eggs in the cell, repeating the cycle. Similar scavenger mites have been found associated with a variety of Sphecidae and Eumenidae in North America. Evidently they do not harm the wasps or their progeny in any way. Possibly those that attach themselves to males are "out of luck," as they will generally have little chance to gain access to a new nest.

Certain mites are properly regarded as cleptoparasites, as they destroy the wasp egg or larva and develop on the prey in the cell. One such mite, measuring half a millimeter long when fully grown, has the imposing name *Lackerbaueria krombeini*. This mite attacks several species of aphid-predators that nest in linear cavities in wood. The immature mites gain access to nests by attaching themselves at random to the bodies of adult wasps. They drop off in freshly provisioned cells, pierce the egg of the wasp, then grow to maturity on the aphids in the cell. In this case the next generation of mites cannot very well attach themselves to the cocoon, so it is assumed that they simply wait until the wasp emerging in an adjacent cell passes through on its way out of the nest, then attach themselves quickly. Presumably the mites in the innermost cells, or in nests in which all cells were infested, will have problems attaching to a host. Since borings in wood are sometimes cleaned out and reutilized by other wasps, some mites may gain access to a host by simply waiting in the old nest.

Mites of the genus *Vespacarus* may be regarded as true parasites of wasp larvae, as they suck their blood without causing their death. These mites attack various twig-nesting Eumenidae, each eumenid appearing to have its own species of *Vespacarus*. The mites feed by puncturing the integument of the larva or pupa, but the wasp nevertheless develops normally. When the molt to the adult stage occurs, the mites are cast off with the old integument, but they soon climb back on the adult, where they congregate in special grooves or acarinaria (Fig. 119). When an infested female begins to nest, the mites drop off and grow to maturity and lay their eggs in the new cell. It is said

FIG. 119. A eumenid wasp, *Stenodynerus fulvipes,* ready to emerge from its cell in a trap nest. The wasp bears many mites (*Vespacarus fulvipes*) in the acarinarium on the second abdominal tergite (arrow). (Krombein, 1967).

that the mites that gain access to the cells are all females, but that these females first produce males which mate with their mothers; the latter then lay female-producing eggs on the wasp pupa.

A still more remarkable mite-wasp relationship occurs between *Kennethiella trisetosa* and its host, the eumenid wasp *Ancistrocerus antilope.* This wasp has acarinaria on its propodeum, just anterior to its abdomen. Curiously, freshly emerged females are invariably free of mites, although the males have the acarinaria crowded with them. It appears that the female wasp larvae search out and eat the mites in the cell before they spin their cocoons, but the males do not. However, mites carried on males cannot reach new cells, and they have developed a remarkable method of transferring to the females before the latter begin nesting. When a male mates, the mites in his acarinaria respond by suddenly streaming down his abdomen and into the genital chambers of both male and female. Those in the genital chamber of the female are admirably poised for entering a new cell at the time of oviposition, while those in the male's genital chamber may gain access to a female at another mating. This remarkable process of "venereal transmission" of mites was first elucidated by Kenneth Cooper, who has the somewhat dubious distinction of having had the genus of mites named after him.

There is no question that mites such as these cannot exist apart from their host and that they do not harm their host in any important way. But how does it happen that the wasps have evolved special integumental pockets which serve to harbor the mites? Have the mites become necessary to the wasps? Do the wasps benefit in some subtle way that we cannot detect? We have only begun to fathom some of the problems of the many associations between these two very different kinds of arthropods.

Other Enemies and Associates of Wasps

Undoubtedly spiders capture a good many of the smaller wasps, although perhaps not many of the larger ones. Jonathan Swift once compared laws to spider's webs, since they "catch many small flies, but let wasps and hornets break through." Considering the great many wasps that use them as prey, the spiders may, on the balance, fare rather badly with respect to wasps. Probably some of the crab spiders, which lurk in flowers and seize various insects that visit them for nectar, are the most successful predators on wasps.

Insects other than those we have mentioned may also serve as enemies of wasps. For example, several species of moths have been found infesting *Polistes* nests, some feeding as larvae on the nest itself, others apparently as parasitoids of the wasp larvae. The larvae of certain ant lions (Neuroptera) are reported as enemies of adult *Bembix* sand wasps in Japan; these formidable larvae hide in the sand near nest entrances and grasp the flies being brought in by the wasps—or occasionally the wasp itself. Ants are major enemies of wasps, both on the ground and in trees and bushes, and may carry off the prey and the wasp larvae and pupae if they gain access to a nest. Ants are especially abundant in tropical forests, and here one finds many wasps nesting in pedicellate nests in trees rather than in hollow twigs or in the ground. A nest suspended from a pedicel is effectively removed from the path of ants patrolling the branches and leaves, and it is probable that a few guard wasps or possibly secretions on the pedicel can often repel invading ants (see Chapter V).

There are, of course, a few wasps that prey upon ants, just as there are some that prey upon other wasps (Chapter II). We may summarize the relationships of wasps with other arthropods by saying that they are complex and often unpredictable. Undoubtedly ants, mites, parasitic flies, cuckoo wasps, and other enemies and associates have, in the course of time, exerted strong influences on the evolution of the behavior patterns of wasps. Many details of nest structure, including various closures and partitions, accessory burrows, pedicels, and so forth, have probably been molded by biotic factors. Indeed, sociality may have originally been selected because of the value of having a "guard" at the nest at all times, and at a later stage because of the effectiveness of a swarm of well-armed workers in repelling natural enemies of all kinds.

We have thus far said nothing about vertebrate animals as enemies of wasps. It hardly needs emphasizing that even large predators quickly learn to treat the nests of social wasps with respect. However, various small mammals occasionally unearth the nests of gregarious non-social ground-nesters, and skunks are even adept at cleaning out the nests of yellow jackets, apparently during the night when the workers are sluggish and disoriented. Certain tropical bats also attack the nests of social wasps at night, as mentioned in the previous chapter. But by and large the aerial nests of social wasps are immune to attack by vertebrate predators.

Birds, to be sure, are major predators on insects, but most of them do not often include wasps in their diet. The few exceptions are chiefly flycatchers; for example, kingbirds have been seen perching near nesting aggregations of *Bembix* and picking off both females and males as they fly about the nesting area. However, young birds of most species quickly learn that wasps are relatively unpalatable and that they sometimes sting. Since birds have excellent vision and seek their prey via visual cues, it is not surprising that wasps have evolved color patterns which birds quickly learn to associate with non-edibility (warning or "aposematic" patterns), that wasps and other unpalatable insects have come to share certain common patterns (Müllerian mimicry), and that a variety of fully palatable insects also share these same "wasplike" patterns (Batesian mimicry). In fact, the coloration of wasps and many other insects can be understood only in this context, and it will pay us to take a closer look at some of these color patterns.

Aposematic and Mimetic Patterns

The most common warning pattern of wasps is a series of yellow bands against a dark background, a pattern characteristic of several species of yellow jackets and variously developed in many solitary Sphecidae and Eumenidae, even in a few Pompilidae, Tiphiidae, and Sapygidae. Gerhard Mostler has shown that birds do in fact learn to reject yellow jackets and that thereafter they also reject other insects bearing similar patterns. It is obviously advantageous for several wasps to adopt a common pattern which birds will have occasion to learn quickly and to relearn periodically (rather than a variety of different patterns). Other insects, including palatable ones, will gain protection from predators to the extent that they simulate the color pattern, flight behavior, and other features of these well-protected models. Mostler's experiments showed that after experiencing several yellow jackets, his birds rejected a high percentage of certain hover-flies bearing very similar patterns, a somewhat lower percentage of flies resembling the models less closely. However, if the mimics were presented *before* the models, they proved highly palatable, and if wasps were then presented they were attacked much more often than if they were presented first. The matter of warning coloration and mimicry has been discussed by Adolf Portmann in another volume in this series (*Animal Camouflage,* 1959), and Portmann has figured several insects that bear the black-and-yellow bands so characteristic of certain wasps (his figures 83 and 84).

In North America, there are not only many solitary wasps, beetles, and other insects that have a generalized resemblance to social wasps (including some of the cono-pid and asilid flies we mentioned earlier in this chapter), but several that bear a very striking, detailed resemblance to wasps. For example, the hover-fly *Spilomyia hamifera* (family Syrphidae) has a pattern of yellow stripes approximating our common yellow jackets very closely. In fact, Albro Gaul has demonstrated that the wings of this fly beat at a rate of 147 strokes per second, while those of *Dolichovespula arenaria* beat at 150 strokes per second. Thus the resulting hum is virtually identical in these two quite unrelated insects (something between D and D♯), a phenomenon that Gaul refers to as "audio mimicry." While *Spilomyia hamifera* is so effective a mimic of yellow jackets that humans (and doubtless birds) are constantly deceived, its close relative *Spilomyia fusca* is an equally striking mimic of the common bald-faced hornet (Fig. 120).

In the tropics, aposematic and mimetic patterns centering about social wasps become striking almost to the point of incredibility. Virtually all the social wasps share their color patterns, either in a general way or in great detail, with other social wasps and with a variety of solitary wasps, parasitoid Hymenoptera, flies, beetles, leafhoppers, moths, and so forth. The stinging or unpalatable members of these complexes are regarded as Müllerian mimics, the palatable members as Batesian mimics. However, in many cases we do not know the degree of palatability, and in fact it is probable that different predators

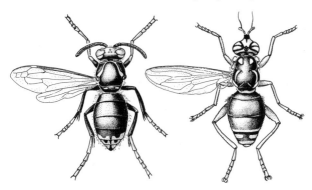

FIG. 120. A worker bald-faced hornet (left) and its mimic, the fly *Spilomyia fusca* (right).

react differently to various wasps and their mimics. The color pattern of any one social wasp may vary geographically, and when it does various mimics vary with it, some mimic different models, and other mimics enter the complex. The taxonomy of many of the insects of Central and South America is still incompletely resolved, and insofar as mimicry of social wasps is involved, it is not likely to be fully resolved until the wasps themselves have been studied much more thoroughly.

Not all these complexes involve yellow-and-black patterns. Among the most ubiquitous and aggressive social wasps of the American tropics are species of *Parachartergus,* several species of which are black and have dark wings which are abruptly whitish on their outer third. This pattern is copied by several other social wasps and also by several solitary eumenids, a spider wasp, at least one digger wasp, and a large chalcid wasp. A species of stingless bees, several flies, and several day-flying moths also share this unusual color pattern. Joseph Bequaert, for many years the leading authority on the American social wasps, listed twenty-eight species of insects as bearing a close resemblance to the "honey wasp" *Brachygastra lecheguana;* nine of these were Eumenidae, two Sphecidae, fifteen bees, one a chalcid wasp, and one a soldier fly. Dr. Bequaert preferred to call this an example of "homeochromy" (color similarity, with no adaptive implications), but enough experimental work has now been done with similar cases to justify the use of the word mimicry—though admittedly it would be desirable to study each case individually.

Not all mimetic complexes necessarily center upon social wasps. Some of the larger solitary wasps have a violent sting combined with aposematic coloration. The best example in the Americas is provided by pompilids of the genus *Pepsis*, the so-called tarantula hawks, many of which have bluish bodies and bright orange wings. Spider wasps of several other genera have members with this same color pattern, though not all are as large as *Pepsis* (several species have subspecies with black wings in the eastern United States, replaced by subspecies with orange wings in the southwestern states and Mexico, where orange-winged *Pepsis* are abundant). Large spider wasps of the genus *Hemipepsis* occur in many parts of the globe and have various color patterns, but only in southwestern North America do they have orange wings—a signal of unpalatability shared by many Müllerian *Pepsis* mimics also found there. Batesian members of this complex include several large flies of the family Mydidae which not only have the bluish bodies and orange wings of *Pepsis* but a strikingly similar manner of flight. Certain day-flying moths also share this color pattern, as do several beetles. Perhaps the most remarkable *Pepsis* mimic is a long-horned grasshopper which not only has the appropriate color pattern but is said to flit about on flowers in a wasplike but most ungrasshopperlike manner.

We have mentioned the brilliant aposematic colors of Mutillidae, or "velvet ants" earlier in this chapter, and it is not surprising to learn that a few Pompilidae have mutillidlike coloration combined with wing-bands which are disruptive so that when the wasp is walking it appears superficially to be wingless, like a female mutillid. Other pale, slender species with banded wings are probably ant mimics. In these cases the mimicry is often confined to the female sex (as it often is in butterflies), the males having a non-mimetic coloration characteristic of that genus. However, several spider wasps are now known which are "dual mimics," that is, the females enter one mimetic complex and the very different-looking males an entirely different one.

The most striking case of dual mimicry involves several South American members of the genus *Chirodamus* in which the females are bluish-bodied, orange-winged *Pepsis*-mimics (as are both sexes of some other species of *Chirodamus*). But in this case the males have evolved an elaborate black, yellow and reddish pattern, and pale wings, making them very like certain social wasps of the genera *Mischocyttarus* and *Stelopolybia* occurring commonly within their range. Since the females spend most of their time on the ground hunting for spiders, it is apparently to their advantage to adopt a common pattern with species of *Pepsis* and other genera occurring there. On the other hand, the males spend most of their time flying about in vegetation seeking honeydew or engaging in prenuptial flights, and in these places there are many foraging worker social wasps with a yellow, black, and red pattern. A number of Ichneumonidae as well as other solitary wasps occurring here also share this same pattern.

Still another case involves members of the pompilid genus *Austrochares*, in which the females have a black-and-red pattern common to a great many ground-inhabiting wasps, while the males mimic social wasps (Fig. 121). However, the model of the males is different from the previous case, for the males have a bright yellow spot on the center of the back of the thorax, as is characteristic of the social wasps *Polybia occidentalis* and several closely related species. In this instance the male is polymorphic, having several color forms, each of which mimics a different member of the *occidentalis* complex. Such detailed resemblance of males to several models different from that of the female is unique.

Although only a few males are involved in dual, sex-limited mimicry, many share the aposematic or mimetic patterns of the females and thereby gain protection from

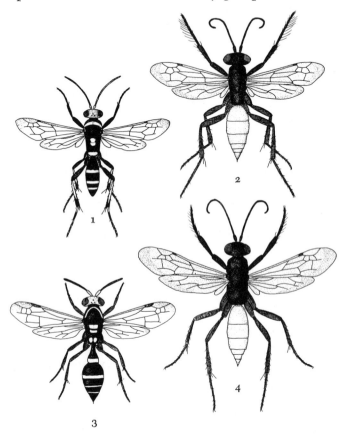

FIG. 121. Dual mimicry in the South American spider wasp *Austrochares gastricus.* Upper two figures (1 and 2) show the mimics (male and female *Austrochares*), lower two figures the models. 3 is a worker social wasp, *Polybia parvula ruficeps,* 4 a female spider wasp, *Dicranoplius satanus.* (Evans, 1969).

predators. Although male wasps cannot sting, as a matter of fact many of them respond with "stinging" movements of the abdomen which are easily demonstrated by simply picking one up in one's fingers. Not all male wasps, but a great many, have a "pseudo-sting," that is, an apical spine or spines that are capable of pricking the skin. The "pseudo-sting" is often a modified last abdominal sternite, but in the Vespoidea it consists of long, sharp prolongations of the genitalia themselves (Fig. 122). This stinging behavior of the males, combined with a lack of palatability, may be nearly as effective in reinforcing the protective color signals as the sting of the females. Pseudo-stings have evolved independently in many different groups of wasps, suggesting that they do, in fact, serve an important function in prolonging the life of the male and that it is advantageous for the male to live a long life. In a few species in which the male has a large pseudo-sting, there is evidence that mating does occur several times over a period of weeks (e.g., in *Steniolia obliqua*), but in other cases it appears that most if not all mating occurs within the first few days of adult life (e.g. in *Bembix*). This leads us to suggest an alternate function of long-lived males possessing pseudo-stings and sharing a common aposematic or mimetic pattern with the female: by doubling the number of protectively colored models, the wasps more effectively outnumber palatable mimics such as conopid and syrphid flies. Thus birds attacking insects of this pattern more frequently receive a sting or pseudo-sting and less frequently associate a "good meal" with this color pattern.

Study of the significance of colors, forms, and behavior patterns of insects is still in its infancy. Many factors other than mimicry are, of course, involved. In the case of wasps and many other wasplike insects, the significance of mimicry has not, however, been fully appreciated. A great many wasps are simply black in color—for example, many Tiphiidae and perhaps the majority of Pompilidae. Yet we

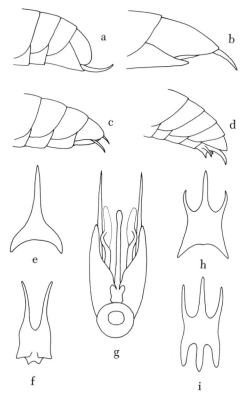

FIG. 122. Pseudo-stings of male wasps. *a. Tiphia* (Tiphiidae) in
side view, showing a somewhat hooked pseudosting formed by the
last abdominal sternite. *b. Sphecius,* the cicada killer, a wasp of
quite a different family (Sphecidae) but also having a pointed,
projecting apical sternite. *c.* A mutillid wasp, *Timulla* (Mutillidae),
having a two-pronged pseudosting formed by the parameres of the
genitalia (as in *g*). *d.* A digger wasp, *Steniolia* (Sphecidae) having
a 4-pronged pseudosting formed by the apical sternite. *e.* Last
abdominal sternite of *Microbembex* (Sphecidae), dissected from
the body (point of pseudosting upward) (similar to that of *a* and
b). *f.* Last abdominal sternite of *Trypoxylon* (Sphecidae), a two-
pronged pseudosting. *g.* Genitalia of *Eumenes* (Eumenidae), in
which the parameres are in the form of a double pseudosting.
h. Stictiella (Sphecidae) and *i. Campsomeris* (Scoliidae), two unrelated wasps both having a three-pronged pseudosting formed
from the apical sternite (points of pseudosting upward).

would suggest that "blackness" plus "wasplike behavior" themselves constitute a signal of avoidance to many predators. This is probably why so many of our common spider wasps are black and why at least one syrphid fly, *Xylota chalybea,* is not only glossy black like a spider wasp but walks along flickering its wings in precisely the same manner as a pompilid.

In the final analysis, we may say that biotic factors in the broad sense—prey, parasites, predators, even such things as nectar sources and available trees and cavities in wood, soil types, and so forth, have all played a role in molding not only the behavior patterns but also the structures and colors of wasps. In a sense a wasp, like any other living thing, is a reflection of all the environmental factors that have influenced it, past and present. The unraveling of such chains of cause and effect is perhaps the most fascinating game we are privileged to play in our own all-too-short life cycles.

Suggested Readings

DUNCAN, C. D.   *A Contribution to the Biology of the North American Vespine Wasps.* Stanford, Calif., 1939.

EBERHARD, M. J. W.   *The social biology of polistine wasps.* Univ. Mich. Mus. Zool., Misc. Publ. 140: 1-101, 1969.

EVANS, H. E.   *Wasp Farm.* New York, 1963. *The Comparative Ethology and Evolution of the Sand Wasps.* Cambridge, Mass., 1966.

IMMS, A. D.   *A General Textbook of Entomology.* 9th edition, revised by O. W. Richards and R. G. Davies. London, 1957.

KEMPER, H. AND E. DÖHRING   *Die sozialen Faltenwespen Mitteleuropas.* Berlin, 1967.

KROMBEIN, K. V.   *Trap-nesting Wasps and Bees: Life Histories, Nests, and Associates.* Washington, 1967.

MALYSHEV, S. I.   *Genesis of the Hymenoptera and the Phases of their Evolution.* London, 1968.

OLBERG, G.   *Das Verhalten der solitären Wespen Mitteleuropas.* Berlin, 1959.

RICHARDS, O. W.   *The Social Insects.* London, 1953. Harper Torchbook, New York, 1961.

RICHARDS, O. W. AND M. J. RICHARDS   *Observations on the social wasps of South America (Hymenoptera, Vespidae).* Transactions of the Royal Entomological Society of London, 102: 1-170, 1951.

ACKNOWLEDGMENTS

Grateful acknowledgment is made for permission to use the following copyright illustrations:

H. E. Evans, *The Accessory Burrows of Digger Wasps. Science,* 152: 465-471, 22 April 1966. Copyright 1966, American Association for the Advancement of Science. Figs. 58, 59.

H. E. Evans, *The Comparative Ethology and Evolution of the Sand Wasps.* Harvard Univ. Press, Cambridge, Mass. Copyright 1966 by the President and Fellows of Harvard College. Figs. 13, 20, 24, 50.

H. E. Evans, *Predatory Wasps.* Copyright 1963, Scientific American, Inc. All rights reserved. Figs. 4, 32.

K. V. Krombein, *Trap-nesting Wasps and Bees: Life Histories, Nests, and Associates.* Copyright 1967, Smithsonian Institution Press. Figs. 64, 118, 119.

F. E. Kurczewski, and N. F. R. Snyder, *Evolution of Cliff-Nesting in Digger Wasps.* Copyright 1968, New York State Conservation Department. Fig. 41.

G. Olberg, *Das Verhalten der solitären Wespen Mitteleuropas.* Copyright 1959, Deutscher Verlag der Wissenschaften, Berlin. Figs. 56, 63, 103.

N. Tinbergen, *The Study of Instinct.* Copyright 1951, Oxford University Press. Figs. 34, 47.

We would also like to express our thanks to the following persons for permitting us to use several unusually interesting unpublished photographs: W. D. Hamilton, Robert Jeanne, Karl V. Krombein, László Móczár, Philip F. Torchio, and Richard F. Trump. W. D. Hamilton and Robert Jeanne also permitted us to use some of their as yet unpublished observations on South American social wasps.

Glossary

acarinarium	groove or pouch in the exoskeleton housing symbiotic mites (Acarina)
aedeagus	male intromittent organ
aposematic	serving to warn
clypeus	portion of the face just above the mouthparts
coxa (-ae, plural)	basal segment of the leg
crop	dilated portion of the foregut just behind the esophagus
diapause	a period of arrested development, usually accompanied by inactivity
extrafloral nectary	nectar-producing organ found on some portion of a plant other than the flower
hibernaculum	cavity or enclosure serving as a hibernation place
honeydew	liquid discharged from the anus of certain plant-feeding insects
labium	"lower lip" of the mouthparts
larviposition	depositing of larvae which have hatched from eggs within the mother
maceration	chewing without ingestion of the chewed material
malaxation	squeezing or chewing of material accompanied by ingestion of juices
Malpighian tubules	excretory tubules arising near the anterior part of the hindgut and extending into the body cavity
maxilla (-ae, plural)	one of a pair of mouthpart structures posterior to the mandibles
meconium	a hard pellet of fecal material discharged by a mature larva into its newly-spun cocoon

oviposition	depositing of eggs
palpus (-i, plural)	a segmented process on a labium or maxilla of the mouthparts
paramere	one of a pair of lateral structures extending beyond the aedeagus of the male genitalia
parasitoid	predatory organism whose immatures slowly consume their host, eventually causing its death; contrasted with a parasite, which does not usually kill its host
pecten	a comblike series of spines lining the outer side of the front tarsus
pheromone	a substance secreted by an animal that influences the behavior of another individual of the same species
proleg	fleshy abdominal leg of a larva
propodeum	the posterior portion of the thorax, which is actually the first abdominal segment united with the thorax
pseudopod	a false leg, formed by a fleshy projection from any part of the body (cf. proleg)
puparium (-ia, plural)	pupal case formed by the handening of the last larval skin
pygidium	flat plate on the upper side of the tip of the abdomen
spermatheca	a saclike structure in which the female receives, and often stores, the sperm
spinneret	a structure, usually fingerlike in shape, which serves as an outlet for silk
sternite	ventral (lower) integumental plate of an abdominal segment
symbiont	an organism living in close association with another to their mutual benefit
tarsus (-i, plural)	terminal segment of the leg
tergite	dorsal (upper) integumental plate of an abdominal segment
trophallaxis	mutual exchange of materials between individuals of the same species

Index